SILENT
GUARDIAN

SILENT
GUARDIAN

TODD AVERETT

Copyright © 2020 by Todd Averett.

ISBN   Softcover   978-1-950596-66-9

All rights reserved. No part of this book may be reproduced or transmitted in any form or by any means, electronic or mechanical, including photocopying, recording, or by any information storage and retrieval system without express written permission from the author, except in the case of brief quotations embodied in critical reviews and certain other non-commercial uses permitted by copyright law.

Printed in the United States of America.

To order additional copies of this book, contact:
Bookwhip
1-855-339-3589
www.bookwhip.com

CONTENTS

Acknowledgment 11

Chapter One   The Wake-Up Call 13

Chapter Two   How the Dream Started 22

Chapter Three   "The Meeting"—Forming the Team 30

Chapter Four   Training Time 46

Chapter Five   Teamwork 54

Chapter Six   Grass Creek and the Omaha Calls 59

Chapter Seven   One of Our Own 66

Chapter Eight   The Reason 71

To Lisa and my mom and dad,
Jessie and Georgia Brooks

It takes a special kind of person to be a volunteer;
some of the traits are selflessness, commitment, and love of
human life and willingness to help a fellow person in the struggles
of life at a moment's notice. I know what it feels like to have your
life in your partner's hands. We have a bond that many people have
never experienced because we know what each other has to lose.

ACKNOWLEDGMENT

PEOPLE DO NOT get to where they are without some very important people in their lives to support and push them even when they don't think they need it. I am grateful to all my friends and family who have helped me along my journey through life with laughter and helpful tips that made it a lot easier. I would not be who I am if I had not listened to them. To my mom and dad, who taught me that love and hard work does pay off and will get you far in life and to have fun in the process. Growing up was tough, and even though we didn't have a lot, I felt like the richest boy in the world.

THE WAKE-UP CALL

THE PAGER TONES out and brings me out of a deep sleep. "Lumpkin firemen, we have a fire on main street, time out two twenty."

I roll over and sit up on the side of the bed and grab my socks and put them on. I then grab my glasses and step in to my turnout boots and pants and pull them up and pull the suspenders up and over my shoulders and turn back to look at the warm bed. I just got in a few hours ago.

I spot Ryan, my two-year-old, and I see he has climbed into bed with Lisa and me in the middle of the night. I pull the covers back up over him and tuck him back in, then I tiptoe out of the bedroom and try not to wake up Lisa for she will have to get ready for work in a few hours. We just got in bed sometime around eleven. Dustin's Little League baseball game ran a little late, and we stopped by Burger King to grab some supper before heading home. I then had the chore of getting Ryan, my youngest son, to bed, and he is in the terrible twos, so that is no easy task. I walk down the hall, and as I pass Dustin's room, I peek inside to check on him. Dustin's my oldest son, but at seven years old, he is a very smart little man and always reminds me that he worries about me every time I go to a fire, but I remind him that Daddy is not alone; I have the other firemen to help take care of me, and I help take care of them.

As I enter the living room, I grab my truck keys and my radio off the dining room table. And then I look toward the kitchen and the time on the microwave oven is two twenty-two. I open the front door and step out on the front porch and close the door behind me.

I turn my radio on as I head toward my truck, and I radio in to dispatch, "Firemen one-zero-eight en route," and Mrs. Mattie answers me back, "Ten- four." It's a cool Friday morning, about fifty-six degrees, and with a slight breeze. It is a little chilly. There are not too many stars in the sky for it is a little cloudy, but the moon is full, and I can see without my flashlight. I reach my truck and open the door and get in and crank up the engine. I pull out of the driveway onto the county road and turn my headlights and my red-'n'-white courtesy lights to and head toward town.

I live about seven miles outside of town, on old Eufaula Highway, but I will make the Lumpkin City speed limit sign in about five minutes. I'm off-work today. I work on site at the local paper mill for a union electrical company. The electrical company has worked on site since 1965 when the mill was built. My boss Dwight Baker is a great guy, and at thirty-three, he is a good supervisor and friend. We are on a four ten-hour days. That way we have a three-day weekend, and we all like that because it lets us spend more time hunting or fishing with our kids in the summertime. Dwight, which we call him Do-Right, is the kind of boss you hope you end up working for, and I've known him and his family for nine years, and I'm glad to call them friends of mine.

Welch Electric is a great company that I have worked for the past ten years. And the owner is one of a kind. He takes care of us, and if we need anything to get the job done, he wastes no time or expense to get us what we need. They have helped me in the past with donations to our fire department, and if I am late to work because of a fire, they help me with my hours too. I will make up my lost sleep later on today, but for now, it's all business and I focus on the job at hand.

I turn on to Main Street and radio Mrs. Mattie for any updates on the fire and who is responding and if anybody is heading to the station to get the fire engine. Before she can answer me, Dan comes over the radio and tells me, "I've got the engine and Chief has the tanker, and he has already left and I will be en route in a couple of minutes."

I pass the courthouse and look toward the station just in time to see Dan pulling out from the station with the engine, so I continue onto the fire. Rusty's pickup pulls out in front of me from one of the side streets, so I fall in line behind him, and we head toward the fire. As we get closer to the house, I can see the flames from the house, and they are reaching high above the trees. It is very smoky in the street, so I slow down not to miss the driveway.

Rusty pulls in to the driveway, and I follow him in, and we pull out of the way so Dan can bring the engine into the yard close to the house. I get out and grab my turnout jacket and helmet from the back seat and put them on. Rusty is doing the same in front of me. I open my toolbox and grab my SCBA (self-contained breathing apparatus); it weighs about thirty-five pounds, and I sling it on my back and fasten it in the front. I grab my mask and clip it on the front of my jacket till later. I reach back in the toolbox for my axe and head toward the front of the house where Chief has backed the red tanker. Rusty then heads over to help Dan get the engine set up.

I also see a glimpse of Mike as he pulls in the driveway in his police car. He is a police officer that is on duty tonight, and I hear him as he radios Dan to let him know that he is pulling the hose off the back and is heading to hook it up to the hydrant, and he will be waiting for his signal to turn it on.

Dan starts getting the engine ready and then gives him the signal that he is ready and the hose is charged. Mike comes up to the engine and Rusty helps him get geared up, and then they head around to the other side of the house. As I approach the front of the house, Chief has an inch-and-a-half hose and is trying to knock down the flames. He is only in his regular cloths, so I yell at him, "Chief, let me have the hose so I can get a little closer." With my turnout suit on, I get closer, but I can still feel the heat, and it is almost blistering even with the gear on. Chief says OK and informs me that no one is inside so I need to be careful.

I put my mask on and turn my air on, and I take the hose from him and move to the left side of the house where the fire has already come out through the walls and roof. So at this point, it is going to be a containment fire, which we call "surround and drown," and that means we will not make an entry but keep it from spreading to any other structure around it. We have fifteen-hundred gallons of water in the tanker, and that will not last anytime. It's not suppressing the fire at all. The water is turning to steam because the fire is so hot. Chief radios me to let me know the water is getting low, and he wants me to move over and give Greg a hand. I shut off the nozzle and pull back to the tanker, and I give the nozzle to

Chief so he can keep an eye on the side of the house. I move to the front door where Greg is at with an inch-and-a-half line from the engine, and he tells me, "We are going to enter the door a few feet and get hold of the fire with Rusty and Mike on the back of the house across from us. We can cut into the fire."

"OK, Greg." He then tells me to take my axe and pry the door open so we can make our entrance in here. But as I push on the door, it comes off in my hands, so I shove it in the house, and Greg opens up the nozzle and follows me inside. I take the door and use it as a shield from the fire and heat, step inside the house, and kneel down as Greg follows me inside and opens up the nozzle.

I prop the door to the side, and then I move into position behind Greg and grab the hose to help advance it into the house. As Greg moves inside with the hose, we can feel the heat and the flames as they roll across the ceiling like clouds in the sky. We get a few feet past the door, and I feel a stream of hot water coming from Rusty's hose as we meet in the middle of the kitchen and turn the fire and start to push it back out where it came from. That way it has nothing to burn, so it slowly starts to go out, and that is when I hear my pressure bell starting to go off, which means I have about five minutes before I'm out of air.

I tell Greg and he motions for me to back out, and as we do, I look above our heads, and the porch is on fire, and the flames are coming through the ceiling where the light fixture was. It looks like a person sticking their hand through a hole, so I tap Greg on the shoulder and show him the fire overhead, and we both back out on to the porch. I tell Greg, "I'm going to use my axe and pull the edge of the plywood down to open it up so you can get some water in there and keep it out from over our heads."

Dan comes over the radio and tells us that the fire has broken through the roof over our heads and we should back off the porch all together. We agree and start to back down the steps and off the porch. As I reach the bottom of the steps, I loosen my face piece and pull it off, and as I start to take a step toward the engine, I just go down on my knees.

Greg shuts off the hose and comes down the steps to help me, and I tell him I'm OK. So he picks me up, and when he lets go of me, I fall flat on my face. I have been trained for heat exhaustion and know how to treat people that get it, but I never knew just how fast it can strike you and take you to your knees.

Chief comes up behind me and helps me walk to the fire engine and sits me on the tailboard of the engine and helps me take my helmet, SCBA, and turnout jacket off, and then he helps me pull my turnout pants down to my boots and sits me under one of the hose connections that are leaking cold water. I let the water run over my head, and it feels good. It is fifty-six degrees outside, and here I am in my boxers and T-shirt, sitting on the back of a fire engine and letting cold water run over my head. It is also filling my boots up, and the water is running out of my pants, and to just think, I love doing this kind of work, and there is nowhere else I'd rather be at this moment but here, helping my friends fight this house fire and make a difference in my community.

As I sit here, I can't lie that warm bed I just got out of would feel great right about now, and after a few minutes, Dan sticks his head around the side of the truck and asked me if I'm better. I just nod my head.

I look up, and here come Woody and Chad, the dream team of the ambulance, my two favorite buds kind of like Laurel and Hardy, great guys to be around. Woody stops and asks me how I'm doing, and when I look up, he says, "I'll give you a little oxygen to help you get the cobwebs out of your head." He sends Chad back to the unit, and he comes back with a small tank and a mask and puts it over my mouth and nose and tells me to relax and breathe.

I sit here for a few minutes, and it feels like my head is going to explode, and the water is running in my mask, so I'm almost drowning. Then Woody comes back from the front of the engine and takes it off and checks me out. "You're good," Woody tells me. "We'll be at the ambulance if I get to feeling bad." And they walk back over to the unit and stand by just in case we need them for an emergency.

I've sat here for about five minutes, so I get up and walk around the side of the engine to see what is going on. Dan asks if I'm OK, and I say yes. Dan then asked me if I feel up to taking over the controls for the pumps so he can check on the guys, and I say, "I got it." I pull my soaked turnout pants back up, and then he lets me know which outlets are open and what pressure they are set on. Then he grabs his helmet and coat and heads up to help Rusty and Mike on the backside of the house where the propane tank is located.

I have yet to understand why we put the propane tanks so close to the house. I know it is to hide it so it doesn't make the yard look bad, but if you have ever seen one blow up, you would put them way back from your house.

It takes another half hour to bring the house under control and extinguish the fire. I bring the pump pressure down on each hose and cut them off as Rusty and Greg pull the hose's back from the house and come over to the engine.

We all sit down for a minute to catch our breath and cool down, and it starts to sprinkle a little rain. I wish it had come a little earlier. Mrs. Jenkins, the owner of the house, comes over with some glasses of cold water and asks if we are thirsty. And she thanks us for putting her house out. She calls us angels for our help. Here is an elderly lady that just lost her house, and instead of worrying where she is going to live now, she is more worried about us. All I can do is say thank you and give her a great big hug. That's the reason I do what I do. It's not for the glory or the fame but to help people like Mrs. Jenkins. I love helping people. I guess I got that from my mom. She has worked in the medical field all her life, and she loves helping people.

Well, a lot of people may think that fighting the fire is the hardest part of this job, but I beg to differ. The real work starts when the fire is a memory and long gone. After we are done with our evaluation of the structure to make sure it is safe, we get out our pike poles and the one-inch attack hose, walk through the fire scene, and make sure that all the hot spots are wet and extinguished so we can leave; we call this "salvage and overhauling."

The worst thing that could happen if we did not do this would be to leave a fire scene and have to return in a few hours and put the fire out again because some hot embers reignited. That makes you look unprofessional and not doing your job the right way. The power and gas companies also show up to cut the power and gas off and make sure it is safe, and we help them too. We then load up the hoses and gear and take it back to the station. We lay the hose out and clean and wash all the sand and soot off them. All the tools are cleaned and stored back in their original place so we know where they are when we need to find them in the dark. We then have to refill our SCBA tanks for the engine and for our personal vehicles for next time and fill both the engine and the tanker back up with water from the hydrant and gas from the Sanger gas station.

That happened to a county not far from us one time. They got back to the station, cleaned everything up, were ready for another call, and went home. They got the next call halfway there but ran out of gas. We had to respond to the scene for them, which is OK because we are only human. They catch our backs as well, and we back them up when they need us too.

I tossed my wet turnout to the back of my truck and put my SCBA and axe back in my toolbox. I will dry them later at home. I walk into the bay of the fire house, and after we finish getting everything back in place, we all sit down and talk about what happened—who did what, if there were any issues that need to be addressed, and how to help better our performances on the next fire call. I get ragged on about my wet boxers, but it is all in fun, and you can't have thin skin around here because they will eat you alive. I love these guys. They are as close to me as my real family. We go hunting and fishing together, our families and kids are friends, and I would go in a burning building for anyone of them as they would do the same for me, and that is what makes us close.

Well, the sun is coming up, and Lisa and the boys will be gone by the time I get to the house, so I can get a shower to wash some of the smoke smell off and maybe even catch a few winks before Lisa and the boys get back today.

Chief catches us before we leave and tells us that he has scheduled some training for us tomorrow at the high school if we can make it. "We will make it around nine o'clock in the morning, and if anybody has Matt's phone number, let him know also." Matt is the other volunteer, but he is a deputy sheriff, and he was tied up on a call-over on the other side of the county. That's our crew, seven volunteer firefighters for the city of Lumpkin, Georgia, with a population of 2,375. I wish we had more, but most people don't think about helping till it happens to them.

Saturday morning, I get up around seven and start breakfast, some grits and eggs and toast, before I leave to meet Chief and the guys at the high school for some fire training. I am trying to be quiet and not wake up Lisa and the boys, but as my luck goes, that doesn't happen. Dustin comes out of his bedroom and says that he wants some Cap'n Crunch, so I fix him a bowl, and we eat breakfast together. After we ate our breakfast, I tell him to go back to his bedroom, watch TV, and keep it down low so Mommy can sleep. I get my stuff together, and before I leave, Dustin tells me that he loves me and to be careful, and I give him a hug.

I pull into the school parking lot and see that Chief is already here with our big red tanker truck; it is a 1974 Georgia Forestry truck that was donated to us when they did not need it anymore. The bad thing is that it puts as much water on the ground as it puts on the fire, but it is Chief's favorite truck.

I pull my truck up close to the school's gymnasium and walk over to the tanker truck, and Chief starts to talk about what we are going to do today and what to start setting out. I help him pull some inch-and-a-half hose off the truck and screw them together to about thirty feet in length. He then pulls a huge nozzle off the truck and tells me to put it on the end of the hose and stretch the hose out toward the school gymnasium.

As I'm doing this, Dan and Rusty arrive and start to help Chief set up the truck and hook it to the hydrant. Mike and Matt come over the hill with the engine, and they turn the lights and siren on as they pull in the parking lot because they know that pisses Chief off when we use them for fun. Mike turns the engine around and backs up next to the pumper so we can hook them together with a six-inch drafting hose later and practice drafting from the tanker. Matt jumps out of the engine and guides Mike as he backs up by the tanker. Matt helps Chief hook the hoses to the pump, and then Chief cranks up the tanker and in-gauges the pump. Rusty, Dan, and I grab the end of the hose and tell Chief that we are ready. He then opens the outlet and the water came out of the truck, under a lot of pressure about one hundred pounds, and the hose begins to bow up like a snake. I just hang on, and it is almost like riding a bucking horse, and it soaked everything including me.

We ended the training day by taking some plywood and cutting ventilation holes out of it to simulate a roof penetration. The object to go up on a roof is to get as much smoke out of a house or building so the rescue team can go in and search for people trapped inside, and believe me, it is a lot easier and safe when you can see. We also tested some new portable extinguishers that we plan to issue to each business in town, and that way, we can introduce ourselves to the owners and answer any questions they might have. Finally, Chief tells us a few things to keep in mind as we approach a fire and to remember that fire consists of three elements—heat, oxygen, and fuel—and to take just one away and it goes out, and as firemen, we use water to cool the heat. We are also taught in training that fire is a scientific phenomenon or like an animal that breathes and destroys everything in its way and will take over if you turn your back on it.

Chief tells us that the smoke and toxic gases in a house fire kill more people than the flames do. The fire uses up the oxygen that you need to breathe and gives off smoke and poisonous gases that even a small amount taken in to your lungs can make you disoriented and drowsy and have a hard time to find your way out of a house. When you are in a house fire, stay low—that is where the air is cooler because the heat at eye level to the ceiling could become a thousand degrees, and at that temperature, the whole room could ignite at once. That is called a flashover. We discuss safety, and if you get lost in a house, follow the wall or the hose out of the house and always stay together. We talk about a few more technical procedures on the pumper and engine and then call it a day. I follow Chief and Mike back to the station so we could lay the hose out to dry and clean the trucks and get them set up for the next call.

HOW THE DREAM STARTED

I GUESS THIS would be a good place to talk about where my love for fighting fire came. It was from my two uncles that were firemen in the city where we lived. Jake and John Henry Brooks became two of my biggest heroes. I was born in Columbus, Georgia, on September 29, 1962, and my father left my mom when I was only nine months old. My mom and my grandmother raised me and my two older brothers in a two-bedroom house, with very little money, but with a whole lot of love and togetherness. With the help of preacher Smith at our church and friends and family, we managed to scrape by, but we were taught to love and to always help one another.

    I will never forget the first time I saw my stepdad. He was very athletic, played softball for a pest control company in Columbus, and worked very hard. My mom quit her job at the hospital where she had worked twelve hours a day to provide for us, and then she got an opportunity to work as a secretary for the same pest control company, make more money, and be home with us more, so she jumped at the chance. My stepdad was a supervisor and talked to her every day, and it wasn't long before they started dating, and when they tied the knot, it was on their birthdays. Yes, that is right. My mom and my stepdad were both born on February 21, one year apart. So Dad just made it easy, and they got married on the same day. Dad said it was easier to just have it all in one day. I was five years old then, and I got a new grandfather and grandmother, four uncles, three aunts, and a lot of cousins to play with, and I was in hog heaven.

I first remember meeting Uncle Henry when he first joined the fire department in Columbus right out of the military. He was six foot four and looked like a giant because he was taller than my dad, and that is why people called my dad little Buddy. Mom said it was because he was named after his dad, but I think it was because of his height. But no matter, he was ten feet tall to me. Uncle Henry worked out of station number 6 in Columbus, and then Uncle Jake, who is a couple of years younger, joined the department and was stationed downtown at number 1. Dad and I went by to see Uncle Henry one day at work, and it was awesome. I got to get in the engine, turned on the lights, put on a set of turnout gear, and climbed on the top of the truck. They even had a basketball goal out back to play while they were not busy, and I enjoyed hanging out with them.

Uncle Henry and a fellow fireman had the chore of making lunch for the entire squad, and I got to eat with all the firemen. I also found out that my dad had grown up with the fire chief. I even meet the two assistant fire chiefs when I started playing Little League baseball. They helped my dad coach my team.

I was on cloud nine. I read books about firemen, and every time I saw a fire truck, it was neat to know some of the guys that worked on them and the lights and sirens. It was then and still is the greatest truck to drive on the road.

One night, when I was about seven years old, we were watching TV, and Dad said he smelled something burning. When he went outside, he saw the house up the street on fire, and he came back in and called the fire department. We went outside the house and stood in the front yard and watched. I stood in disbelief at what was happening. I had seen the older people that lived there but did not know who they were. I stood there watching the fire coming out of the windows and shooting twenty feet in the air, and the smoke was so black that it was scary. Dad ran to the house to help if he could.

We watched as the fire truck came rolling up the street, and the firemen jumped off dressed in their fire suits and put the fire out in no time flat. They looked like knights coming to save the day, and they did. The couple was safe from harm, and when my dad came back down the street, some of the firemen yelled at him, and that was pretty cool. I talked to Dad and told him when I get old enough, I wanted to be a fireman, and he told me that it takes a special kind of person to be a fireman; while everyone is running out of a burning building, you will be running in to risk your life for a stranger, and that is why it is a tough job. Dad also said he would help me when the time comes if that is what I really want to do.

I could not wait to be a fireman. I used the garden hose to practice putting out fires when we washed Mom and Dad's vehicles. I even wrote my senior term paper, "Study of Fire in Our Society," on firemen and got to interview my uncle Henry and some of the firemen, and to hear their accounts of different fires was intriguing. I only got a B, but that was OK, for I was going to become a fireman in a few months and do it for real.

life sometimes has a sick sense of humor; it will knock you down and just laugh at you unless you get up, stand your ground, and fight for what you believe in. I graduated from high school, and three months later, I was in intensive care at the hospital. I guess I should back up just a bit and tell you the whole story of what happened that day.

I was working in the kitchen at the hospital as a part-time porter till the hiring and training started for the Columbus Fire Department. I had that day off. It was a Tuesday, and my cousin and I had been working on my car for the past six months, putting a new motor in and fixing it up. We got the motor reworked and mounted in my 1969 pontiac leMans but could not get it to crank, so we ended up having to take it up the street to let a mechanic at an electrical shop work on the wiring because it had a short circuit in the wiring harness. The mechanic called on Monday, and he said we could come and pick it up on Tuesday morning for he was through with it. Mike, a good friend of mine, came over on Tuesday morning, and we headed up the street to the shop to get my car. And as my luck would have it, the motor would not turn over, so the mechanic said that the small garage across the street worked on carburetors, and I could see if they could help me get it running.

Mike and I ended up pushing my car across the street so the mechanic could take a look at it and find out what was wrong. I had to pour some gas in the tank with an antifreeze jug since I was out. But I didn't even have a funnel, so I spilled some on my hands and the ground and wiped some on my pants in the process. Then the mechanic told me to fill up a quart oil can with gas and sit it on the grill because he would need some to prime the carburetor. I then got inside the car, and when he told me to, I turned the key and tried to crank it up.

Boom! The carburetor backfired and scared the hell out of me because I had just put fifteen hundred dollars in the motor to rebuild it, and I didn't want it to burn up. The mechanic told me to turn it over again, and when it backfired this time, it caught the oil can, and the front of the car was on fire. I saw all the flames and went to help put out the fire, but as soon as I opened the door and got out of the car, the mechanic slung the oil can toward the street away from the car and right at me. The oil can hit me about waist-high, and I went up like a candle. All the gas on my hands and pants ignited, and the only thing I remembered hearing was Dick Van Dyke saying "Drop and roll to put the fire out" from a TV commercial. So down I went, and it took a few minutes to put it out, but it did finally go out. I stood up and everything around me was moving in slow motion. My skin was running off my hand. All the skin on my legs was burnt up to my knees. And all I wanted to do was find some water to put on my hand and cool it off. Mike was yelling that we need to go get my mom and go to the hospital, so he put me in his Baja bug, and we headed toward my house to get my mom.

I didn't remember too much about the next ten minutes, but it had changed my life forever. Mike drove toward my house and then turned on a side street and gave it some gas. I looked over at him and said, "My skin is dripping off my hand and into my lap." And when he turned to look, I caught a glimpse of a yellow truck heading right at us, and then I saw the stop sign and yelled, "Stop sign!"

The next thing I knew was I could not move. It was quiet, everything was white, and all I could think was *Is this what heaven looks like?* I found out later that I had been thrown eighty-seven feet down the road, and the first police officer on the scene said he thought I was dead, so he put a sheet over me to keep any cars from running over me. I don't know how long I laid there till the paramedic pulled the sheet off. As the color came back in my sight, I then saw the paramedics cutting my pants off and putting a cervix collar on me. Then they put me on a backboard and strapped me down. They put me in the ambulance, and as I was waiting to go to the hospital, they slid Mike in beside me. He was also on a backboard, and it looked like half his face was missing.

I looked over and yelled at him, but nothing. I thought he was dead, but after yelling at him the second time, Mike finally looked at me and said, "I wrecked my car." I wanted to reach over and strangle him. His car? What about us?

We're on the way to the hospital. I had second- and third-degree burns. Mike was missing one layer of skin from his nose to his left ear and had glass all in his arms, but he is worried about his *car*. It was a good thing I was strapped down. I, on the other hand, was worried about missing work tomorrow, so that is just as bad.

I work in the kitchen at the hospital as a porter, and Sister lambert is my boss. When I got to the hospital, she came up to the intensive care unit, and as she looked at me, all she said was "Some people just don't know what to do with a day off," and we both laughed. She is a great boss.

Over the next few months, I recovered from the burns, and Mike got his looks back, and we still talk about the wreck to this day whenever we get together. I realized that when you go through life experiences with people, you gain trust in each other as I have found with the volunteers I work with now. The wreck as a whole changed my life and outlook on life. I even sustained some injuries that, at that time, I could not pass the physical test, and that would be the main reason I could not join the city fire department.

I was crushed. My life, or what I was going to do with my life, was over before it even got started. Eventually I moved on with my life, got married to the love of my life, and became an electrician working for my father-in-law. It was a change of life and of location that, as I said, life has a weird sense of humor, but sometimes it does set the record straight and also helps you start again.

I joined a local union in Columbus after a few years in technical school and working for other electrical companies. I started working at a paper mill about thirty miles out of town. The money was good, so Lisa and I decided to move out of the city, buy some land, and build a house. After twelve years of marriage, and with a four-year-old son and one on the way, it was a big transition from a big city to a small town south of Columbus. But we felt it was a good move.

The small town of Lumpkin, Georgia, is where it is like stepping back in time to Mayberry, and you might even get a glimpse of Sheriff Taylor.

Lumpkin was, at one time, the farthest southern outpost and built on top of a hill so you have to come up a hill on all four sides for protection from Indians years ago. The town was incorporated in 1829 and has a population of about two-thousand people. It has a courthouse that sits on a square with all the shops around it like Junior's thrift shop, Sanger's gas station, or Randy's gas station. The sheriff department looks like an old castle right off the square, but one of the biggest attractions in Stewart County is a place called Westville.

Westville opened in 1970 and is considered the "gates to the past." It is made up of a lot of old buildings that date back to the early 1850s, and it has tourists and school kids that come to enjoy stepping to the way it was back in the day. I went there once, and you can see the way blacksmiths shoe horses and watch how they used to cook in old brick ovens. It's a great place to spend the day. There is even a place called the "Little Grand Canyon" just up the road, and my older brother Chester lives there, so it was no wonder I came to Lumpkin.

I worked in construction for a living, and as a lot of people know, that can sometimes be seasonal work at best. That being said, my dad always told me that a man has to provide for his family and keep a roof over their heads and food on the table and, in my case, diapers on my son's behind. As for picking Lumpkin, Chester moved there about five years before I did, and he said it is a good place to live. I have always favored Chester as he and I are about the same when it comes to working hard, doing what you love to do, and being the first one to lend a hand to someone in need.

Chester is an antique restorator and can tell you anything about wood— what kind it is or what stain to put on it to make it look good. He repairs a lot of early-1800s furniture and works for Mr. Halliday. Mr. Halliday buys antiques from England and has them shipped over in containers to his warehouse here in Lumpkin, where he sells to other local antique dealers in the area. Chester runs his shop, where they restore any furniture that is broken or needs some fixing up in order to sell, which he does, and they receive a container every other month during the summer. Chester works until two o'clock in the morning, sometimes to make some extra money, and I'd be right there with him, making a little extra money too. The reason for the late hours is because Chester is the kind of person that can do about anything. He's a very good handyman, and he is also the bail bondsman for Stewart County, so the only time he can do some work for himself is when everyone else is asleep. Chester also opened up a refurnishing store up on the square for himself across from the sheriff's office to try and make a go of it. I helped him wire the place up as it was an old store that had been closed for years, so we got it for very little rent, and we fixed it up all by ourselves.

It was here that I was working one night, staining some kitchen chairs, when Ray walked in and introduced himself as chief of the volunteer fire department here in Lumpkin. He works as a guard at the prison camp during the day and is the fire chief at night. I guess the only way to describe Chief is that he is one of a kind. He is short, about five feet eight inches tall, a fireman from the Stone Age, and one of the grumpiest people you will ever meet. I thought that this guy must be hell to work with, but as he gets to know you, he changes and is one of the hardest working guys and very funny, which, in his line of work, helps a lot. After he left, I asked Chester about Chief, and he began to tell me a story he had heard around town about a warehouse fire a few years back.

One day when Chief was responding to a warehouse fire in Richland, which is about eight miles from Lumpkin, Chief took the pumper over there, and as he was approaching the warehouse, all the other volunteers watched as he drove the pumper right into the warehouse. It took about twenty minutes before he put the fire out, and afterward, everyone around told him he was a hero for saving the building and asked him why he drove the truck into the building. All Ray said when questioned was "The brakes failed, and it was getting hot, so I didn't have much choice in the matter. So I put the fire out."

Chester said, "He is a good guy."

When I first moved to Lumpkin, I stayed in an apartment in town two doors up from where Chief lives. There is an alley behind my house that connects all the houses and helps with trash collection. I purchased twenty acres outside of town, and I'm going to build a house on it eventually.

After settling in, I went to the local grocery store that is run by Rusty. Chester introduced me to Rusty. He is a nice guy, about ten years older than me, and his family is from here, and he has been here his whole life. Rusty is very witty and comes across as a hard worker and a family man. His mom, Mrs. Carol, is the cashier, and she is a very funny, kind of like my mom. Angel, his wife, and little Russ are just great people to know. Chester told Rusty that if he needs some electrical work done, then I'm his man. I shook Rusty's hand, then Chester's, and I head back to the shop.

Outside the store, a Lumpkin police car pulled up, and Chester and I walked over to it. As the officer got out and walked over, Chester introduced me to Mike Oats. I shook his hand, and he was a little younger than me, and we talked for a few minutes. He liked baseball and hunting, and he seemed like a great guy.

We got back to the shop, and it's about eight o'clock, so I headed to the house while Chester went inside to get some work done.

A month later Chief came by the shop one night, and we all got to talking about this and that and things going on around the city. Then Chief asked me if I wanted to join the volunteer fire department, and Chester looked at me and said, "I thought you might like that." He knew how I've always wanted to be a fireman and how hard it affected me when I got hurt. Chief looked at me and asked if I wanted to join, and I said yes, not knowing anything about it or what kind of issues I'd soon learn about volunteer firefighting. Chief told me that if I wasn't busy on Saturday, around noon, he would stop by and take me to the station. I told him that I'd be ready.

"THE MEETING"— FORMING THE TEAM

ON SATURDAY, CHIEF picked me up around noon, and we drove over to the fire station, which is a white barn beside the old schoolhouse. I kind of thought at that point what had I gotten myself into, but I wasn't going to run just yet. The barn consisted of two bays, one for the fire engine and one for the tanker truck. I opened the big wooden doors that were held together by a chain and some nails. It was dark and creepy inside, and some of the roof was missing. Chief turned the two fluorescent lights on that don't give off too much light, and we walked around the back of the fire engine. I guessed the first thing we need to do was to find me a set of turnout gear, a helmet, and some boots.

Chief and I started looking around. All the coats and pants were on the floor and dry-rotted. Some were even torn to halves. I tried on about three pairs of boots after making sure there were no critters inside, and I finally found a pair that fits me. I then looked over in the corner, and there was a pair of pants standing up by themselves. We started to laugh about that. I checked two or three helmets, and some either don't have any interior in them, or they were just so old that they have warped and have been discolored. The last one I checked was about the best, and Chief said to get it before anybody else picked it up. "OK" is all I could think to say.

Well, we looked over behind the engine and in some of the compartments to see what was in there and what was not. I didn't see too much stuff in there to work with, and Chief asked me if I saw the axe in the side compartment. I said no. He said, "I told Ed, when he's through chopping down those bushes, to bring it back." He then handed me a pair of blue gloves that were new. I thought that at least my hands will be fine. Chief and I walked around to the driver's side of the engine, and he opened the door, got inside, and set in the driver's seat. He cranked the engine up and let it run till it idled down. Then he showed me how to put the motor in neutral and engage the PTO switch, which controls the pump on the truck to supply water from the hydrant to the hoses; how to flip the lights on and work the radio; and how to use the emergency brakes, which is, as he said, the most important thing. The tools on the truck were few and far between: we had a couple of pike poles, a fire extinguisher, some old hose fittings, about five hundred feet of two-inch hose in fifty-foot sections, and some inch-and-a-half hose of about the same amount. Chief also told me that the fire engine stays in the city limits, but the tanker can go out in the county to back up and help the Georgia Forestry personnel.

We then talked about volunteer fire department training that each member has to go through in order to receive a forty-hour certificate to become a module one firefighter, which is the state standard for all volunteer firefighters. Once I get that, I can be put on the roster and be covered by the state for workman's compensation and life insurance when I go on a fire call.

He also said that he was talking to a new guy that just moved here from South Carolina. The city council was going to make him the assistant fire chief, and his name was Joe McCord. Joe wanted to start having weekly meetings for training and fire business and to recruit some new firemen from the county, but I will let you know when, and I'll also see when the next state training classes are and where.

Well, it was about two o'clock, and Chief told me that when he gets a call from the sheriff's department, he will then call me, and if I'll just walk out to the main road, he will stop so I can jump in. I told him that it sounds great, that I thank him for everything, and that I'll see him later.

When I got home, I told Lisa all about what I and Chief had talked about.

I showed her my helmet and boots, and she just gave me a "what the hell" look and asked me, "Why do you always pick the most dangerous jobs to do? You are an electrician at the paper mill, around all that high-voltage equipment that I have to worry about. And now you are going to be running off in the middle of the night to put out a burning house or God only knows what with nothing but a pair of boots and a helmet! Have you lost your mind? Out here in the county, you can hit a deer or whatever comes out in front of you, and you could end up in a ditch, and that's supposed to be OK. What about Dustin and Ryan? What am I supposed to do if something happens to you? How am I going to go on without you here?"

I was floored. I had never thought about not coming home or thought about her standpoint. It was just a job to me, not life or death. Having children changes the way you look at life, knowing that someone depends on you always. Being there gives you a different perspective. I was now confronted for the first time in my life with the job I've always wanted to do, and the person I wanted to be could kill me. We talked more about it over supper and came to the conclusion that I would not take any chances that might put me at risk. I told her what she wanted to hear because any fireman knows that the job comes with risks, especially if there are kids involved. I guess Lisa knows that I will help a total stranger. She knows how I've always wanted to be a fireman, and that means there are risks.

I guess I will never forget that first phone call. It was a Tuesday morning around two o'clock. I answered the phone, and Elizabeth, Chief's wife, told me that Ray was on his way to get the fire truck, and he would pick me up in a few minutes by the road. I hung up the phone and slipped out of bed, grabbed my blue jeans and socks, and headed to the living room to put them on so as not to wake up Lisa. My boots were in the hall, and so were my helmet and flash light. I slipped them on and opened the front door, trying not to wake Dustin; his bedroom was close to the front door.

I closed the front door behind me and headed toward the street. It was dark that morning, no moon or stars that I could see, but the street light was glowing bright, and I could see how to make my way to the curb. As I was standing there in my regular cloths, and it was cool, the butterflies in my stomach kept me moving until I heard this loud noise come around the corner. And it was chief in the tanker truck.

He slowed to a stop, I jumped in and slammed the door, and away we went. We headed to town, probably waking everybody up along the way as we went, but hey, no need to be quiet. Chief gave me the radio and told me to call and let Mrs. Mattie know that we were en route to the fire. So I yelled to the radio, "Tanker one to dispatch en route to fire."

I heard the dispatcher come over the radio. "Ten-four, tanker one, what is your twenty."

Chief said, "Tell her we are two miles out, headed down the Georgetown highway toward US thirty-nine."

"OK." And I relayed the message to Mrs. Mattie to the best I can.

It was so loud in the cab that I had to hold the radio to my ear, but I can still barely hear anything on the radio. I looked over at the odometer and saw that we were doing seventy miles an hour. Man, we were cruising, and with the fifteen hundred gallons of water in the tank, it would be hard to slow down too quickly. So I reached over and pulled my lap belt over and hooked it up.

I put the radio back up to my ear, and out of the corner of my eye, I caught some blue flashing lights coming up behind us at a very rapid pace. And I heard, "Tanker one, this is one-o-three. I'm coming up on you." I yelled to chief that one-o-three was behind us, and before the Chief could respond, a streak of blue flashing lights blazed past our left-hand side.

Then the Chief said, "That's Matt. He's one of the deputy sheriffs and part of the fire department." And Matt's car disappeared into the darkness. As we topped the next hill, I looked over to my left and saw the fire and how bright the sky was lit up. I got a feeling like I had never felt before in my life. It was a sickening feeling, and I just hoped everybody got out OK.

Chief yelled at me. We're going to turn just up ahead, and he started to gear down. We made the turn and headed up the road toward the huge flame that was lighting up the whole sky. The house was totally engulfed as we turned in the driveway. Chief told me to jump out when he made the stop so he could back up with the back of the tanker facing the house. As Chief was backing up, I met Matt for the first time, and he was a nice guy, about six feet tall. He shook my hand and told me that he wished it was in different circumstances in which we were meeting, but "Welcome to Lumpkin." I just told him thanks.

Chief yelled to me to come and grab the hose and stretch it out toward the house, and as I am doing this, Chief fired up the gas pump on the back tailboard of the tanker. I approached the house, and the water filled the hose up and jerked me a little as I started wetting the grass up to the house, and it hit me in the face like a brick wall. The heat was intense, and it took my breath away, so I knelt down, turned the hose toward the window, and started shooting water through it.

I continued this for a moment or two, and Chief came over and told me, "We don't have a lot of water. Everyone got out safely so just hit the trees and grass to keep it from spreading into the woods." I slowed my efforts and backed up a little to get out of the heat and cool down, and I walked around the side of the house just to keep an eye on the back. We all just stood there watching this nice house burn to the ground, knowing there was nothing we could do to prevent it from happening. A house that was someone's home, someone's dream for the future that they paid money for, that they wanted to grow old in, was now just a pile of ashes, all gone. I looked at the fact that all the pictures of the family, favorite rocking chair, big screen TV, and old memories and collectables are now gone for good.

As I stood there spraying the grass and trees down, I happened to look over by the well house and saw a man standing there with a small boy in his arms and a little girl standing beside him, just staring at what two hours ago used to be their house. I stopped for a minute, and he threw his arm up to wave at me, and all I could do was wave back. Then he went over to a pickup truck, and he put the kids inside. I saw that there were some stuff on the back that he managed to save as he drove off, but I'm just glad they were all safe because you can buy furniture and clothes, but you can't buy a life back.

Chief and I stayed about two hours after everyone else left till the final wall hit the ground and all the fire and ambers were contained, and we knew it wouldn't start up again. The power man and the propane company came out to cut everything loose so no one could get hurt. I rolled up the hose and put it back on the truck, and Chief and I headed back to town.

It was seven thirty, and I had to go to work, but my boss told me if anything came up, I just call and let him know. We pulled the tanker up to a fire hydrant and began to fill the tanker back up for another call, and then Chief dropped me off by my house, and I got ready and headed to work.

On the way to work, all I could think about was the man and his two kids. What do you do when all that you know is gone? You still have to worry about the mortgage payment, the electric bill, the credit card bills, and work or school for the kids. Man, that could drive you crazy, and if someone was injured on top of that, it's unthinkable. I worked ten hours in a daze, wondering if I could have done more to help, or if we could have responded quicker, could we have made a difference by all I have—a pair of boots and a helmet. What if someone was in the house? A child? I hope I never have to be part of a scene like that. Something needs to change, and people need to know what could happen if those events arise.

That night at supper, I looked at Lisa and the boys and thought what we would do if it happened to us, and we talked about it. Lisa asked about the family and if they were OK. And she just said she was glad that no one got hurt. I had to go to the grocery store on Saturday morning to get a few things for supper, and when I walked in to Rusty's, I said hey to Mrs. Carol and grabbed a buggy and headed toward the meat department.

I looked over the ribs and steaks, and Rusty walked up behind me and said, "Hey, Todd, what's up on this early Saturday morning?"

I just laughed and said, "Not too much." But I went to a fire earlier this week, out in the county, and it has been on my mind all week long.

Rusty then told me the name of the family, and the father's family was helping them out. The kids were fine, and they had insurance to take care of everything. "Great" is all I could come up with.

We talked a little more, and then this smaller man with glasses walked up. Rusty turned to him and said, "Todd, I'd like you to meet Joe McCord, our new assistant fire chief, and he works for the city." Joe is a very athletic-looking guy. He is quick with a comeback, so being around construction workers, I like his wit and humor.

I looked at Joe and said, "I'm glad to meet you." And we sure need someone to help organize and train us to deal with fire calls that we respond to. We need better equipment, and all I have is a pair of boots and a helmet. I guess we are an outstanding fire department—standing out in the yard, that is.

Joe agreed and told Rusty and me that he was getting a meeting together for Thursday night, about seven, at the city barn, to discuss what we need to do to get people and equipment for our fire department and that if we know anybody that's interested to tell them too. I left the store thinking that we are going to have a good fire department with more men and women and better equipment to work with.

On Thursday night, I got to the meeting at about six thirty. I like to be early instead of being late and people having to wait on me. Joe and Ray were the next to arrive, followed by Rusty and Mike, and finally Matt. Greg was on a medical call, headed to Columbus on the ambulance, or he'd be here. Joe said we'd wait a few minutes to see if anyone else came up because I told a bunch of people this week about the meeting tonight. We waited a few minutes, and nobody else showed up, so we moved inside the barn and sat around this wooden table with junk piled all around us—not your everyday meeting room.

Chief and Joe started the meeting with letting everyone know that we first needed to be certified with at least module one firefighting, which only Mike and I did not have, and everyone else did. Joe told Mike and me that they had some times and dates of upcoming state training schedules that we could try and get on. He also went on to tell us that we were going to have BLEVE training, which means "boiling liquid expanding vapor explosion," like when dealing with propane tanks or any kind of vehicle wrecks —and yes, we were going to start responding to vehicle wrecks too, which is why we had to get certified in vehicle extrication, hazardous material response..

I will start working on the city council to get some funding for radios and pagers for each one of us, some new turnout gear for everyone, and possibly some SCBAs so we can go into a fire and rescue someone if the need ever arrives to do so. Make no mistake about it, guys. In order to do this, it will take some sacrifices and commitment from everybody as well as corporate and other private donations we can get. Chief and I are going to talk to the city council next week to ask for a one-cent sales tax to possibly get a new fire engine and fire station on the square, which they have been talking about, making Lumpkin the center of the county to keep the ambulance anyway. If they do that, we might include a place for the fire engine too. Well, thanks for coming out tonight, and hopefully, this is the start of something great. We are going to start meeting every second and last Thursday of each month, the second for business and the last for training. So pass it on to anybody that wants to join.

A couple of weeks went by, and I had to go to a neighboring county on Saturday and Sunday for two weeks to get my forty hours of state training done. The chief in Georgetown worked at the paper mill with me, and he let me borrow some turnout gear for training. I was also going around town asking for donations, but pulling alligator teeth would have been an easier chore. I finally went to the hardware store called Frankie's, and this guy Frankie was as nice as anybody in town.

He invited me in, and we talked about what we were doing and the things to come. He knew my brother, and he liked Chester. They do a lot of business together, so he let me know anything that I need; I just have to ask.

I thought about how I was going to do this, and one of the guys I worked with at the mill said, "Have a raffle or sell some barbecue. Everybody likes to win something and eat food."

"Great idea," I replied. I came up with a raffle, used the services of the merchants, cooked some food at the fair on the square, and made some T-shirts to sell with all the merchants on the front and the fire logo of the lVFD (Lumpkin Volunteer Fire Department) on the back.

I walked around town and started talking to the store owners, and they started donating a lot of neat stuff: Randy's gas station gave a free free oil change. The oil company gave "free twenty dollars' worth of gas." There was dinner for two at Snookie's diner. The bank gave one hundred dollars. Then other businesses all started to climb on board too as soon as I told each of them that the other businesses were doing this or that. Nobody in a small town wants to be the one left out.

We raised fifteen hundred dollars, and I even got a shotgun donated to raffle off from Richland gun sales and some T-shirts that we bought for two dollars each and will sell for ten at the fair on the square.

Thursday night was a business night, and we got together at a small diner called Snooky's, and it was better than the old barn. Joe brought the meeting to order at seven o'clock, and in attendance were Rusty, Matt, Mike, Chief, Greg, and me. This was the first time I've meet Greg, so I introduced myself to him. He is a big man, about six-four. He is also the chief of the EMS (emergency medical service). Here in Stewart County and a paramedic on top of that, his dad is a fireman in Columbus, so he has been around the fire service all his life.

Joe started handing out positions and ranks, and I volunteered for the treasurer. I got the rank of probationary fireman since I just got my certification, but Mike got the same, so I'm not alone at the bottom. Greg also got to be an assistant chief with Joe. Matt got a captain's position. And Rusty got a fireman's position. I stood up and told them what I have in the works, and Joe made me the secretary also to keep records of training and supplies. Joe also told us that the city council has a new building in the works, which would double as a council hall and EMS building for the ambulance and two EMTs on duty. They were also adding two extra bays for the engine and tanker, which should only take a month or two to build if all went as planned. Chief told us that he had not heard from anybody else in town interested in joining the fire department; they all just said they don't have time. We were becoming a tight group of firemen, and I'm glad to be part of it. We were dismissed at eight.

A couple of weeks went by, and Joe called me at home and said that for the Thursday night training, we will be meeting at the city barn and to inform everyone to be there at seven to try on some turnout gear that we just got from a volunteer fire department in South Carolina. I told him OK.

I got to the barn around seven, and everybody was already there as I walked inside the barn.

"Good. Everyone is here." Joe said. Then he began to tell us that we had twelve pairs of turnouts, boots, and helmets, and they threw in six SCBAs. "So everyone needs to get a pair of boots, a pair of pants, and a jacket to go together. If you need a helmet, grab one with a skullcap. I'm also going to issue out the SCBAs to the people that will be around town during the day first, and then everyone else. Well, there is only six SCBAs, and I make number seven. Mike is from Lumpkin so it is only fair that he gets one, plus he is a police officer in the city, and if we have a fire, he will need one. I will run the truck outside, which is just important because, as long as they go in, I will keep the wet stuff coming so they can put it on the hot stuff."

We got our gear and tried them on to make sure they fit. Chief was handing out hoods and some gloves. Man, it was like Christmas. I got all my stuff together, and Joe walked over to me and told me that he was going to give me one of the SCBAs. He said, "Chief doesn't need one. He is going to watch the tanker, and let us young men go inside."

Joe then told us that the contractor was going to break ground on the new fire station next week; they want to get it built and moved in before the fair on the square in four months. That's great news. We ended the meeting around eight thirty, and I left with a feeling that this was going to be a great.

Saturday afternoon I got a call from Matt. He said that we had a dog trapped in an abandoned well out past Westville at the Johnsons' farm and, if I could come, help get him free. I said, "Sure, on my way."

I got on the scene. Matt, Mike, and Chief were already there in the woods. I followed a fence line into the woods where they were. On the way, I looked over the fence, and ten feet away was a swing set and some kid toys. As I walked up, Matt was setting up a tripod over the well, so I joined in and we set it up. Then Matt looked at me and asked if I could get some rope and a safety harness from work. I told him I can try. I called my boss at home and asked him if it would be possible to get some rope and a harness from the tool room at work. I then explained our situation and all Do-Right said was "Get what you need."

Matt and I took his squad car and we flew. In no time at all, we were at the mill, and in forty-five minutes, we were back with the rope and harness.

I looked down in the well for the first time, and the dog was at least forty feet down in the well. I'm just glad one of the children didn't fall in. Matt told me that there were abandoned wells all over the county. The forestry used to drill wells to water the new seedling trees when they planted them. They would then just push some dirt over them, but sometimes it didn't fill them in. They just left open holes that vines grew over, and anybody that happened to be alone could fall in.

I helped get Matt in the harness, and Mike hooked the rope to the tripod. I moved back, and when Matt was ready, Mike and I lowered him into the well as Chief kept an eye on him. It took about thirty minutes to lower him down to the dog and pull them both back up to safety. The dog suffered from sore legs and dirt in his eyes. The kids were glad to have him back safely, and the well was filled in once and for all. Matt showed me that one person can make a difference.

I was at work on a Tuesday morning when Joe and Rusty responded to a modular home on Elm Street. It's another name for what us southern people call a double-wide trailer. Mrs. Brown and her son Ronnie were living there together, and he had just got home from working the night shift at the mill, and Mrs. Brown was out of town. Ronny had got a shower and was in the kitchen fixing some breakfast when he smelled some smoke coming from his bedroom. He cut the stove off, and when he looked down the hall, he saw flames coming out of the bedroom. So he grabbed his cell phone, ran outside the house, and called the sheriff's department right away. Mrs. Mattie dispatched the call over the radio, Joe was at Rusty's store, and he and Rusty headed up to the city barn, got the fire engine, and headed to the fire scene.

On the way there, they got a call that Matt was en route and would meet them there. When they arrived at the house, the fire had already broken through to the outside and was engulfing the corner of the house. Joe grabbed the attack hose, and he and Matt entered the house while Rusty stayed outside and manned the fire engine to supply the water pressure. Joe and Matt forced the fire back out of the house. Rusty hit it from the outside with a line, and it was snuffed out in less than fifteen minutes.

This was the first time in Stewart County history that the fire department had ever saved a modular home or trailer, so now we can say that when we respond to a fire, we save more than just a chimney. We can protect property and save lives. I have learned a lot about the fire service in the short time I have been involved with the lVFD. A lot of people know that if you have a fire hydrant close to your house, your home owners insurance is cheaper. Ratings are assigned by ISO, a company that collects and analyzes information on fire protection in small towns and communities all over the United States. The scores range from a one, which indicates great fire protection, to a ten, which indicates that the area's program fails to meet the minimum requirements. Lumpkin is at a nine, and that is something we plan to change, for the betterment of the town and to let people know that we are here to make a difference.

The council hall/ambulance– fire department building would be completed next month and the fair on the square at the end of the month, so we were going to have to work every minute we could to be ready for it.

I talked to a fellow named Bubba, and he would have the T-shirts printed and ready in a couple of weeks. Rusty has ordered the fifty pounds of chicken fingers, one hundred pounds of potatoes for french fries, the three five-gallon cooking oil, and all the condiments to sell at the fair on the square. This event is a yearly tradition where we get hundreds of vendors to set up around the courthouse on the square, and people come from all over to buy crafts, food, and stuff like hot sauces, cloths, and toys. We wanted to sell food in front of the fire station and would answer any questions the people have or just introduce ourselves to the community. I couldn't wait.

We had our end-of-the-month meeting in the new council hall, and as we started the meeting, Chief introduced us to a new man that just moved here from Tennessee and was working at Fort Benning. His name was Dan Simpson, and he was a sergeant in the military. He would like to join us here in the fire department since he already had a module one basic firefighting from the volunteer department he worked at in Tennessee. So I thought he would be a good addition to our town and our department. We all welcomed Dan and told him who we were. He told us that he lived next to Chief, but we wouldn't hold that against him.

I went over the expenses and told them that I have got the gun for the raffle and the tickets were printed and we went over them. "We will sell the tickets for five dollars each. That gets you a half of chicken dinner with three sides and a chance at one of the ten prizes we discussed last meeting. And the mayor will draw the names."

We then went out in the new bays where the trucks were parked, and even with them in here, we still have a lot of room behind the trucks. It was nice. We have a drink machine and plenty of room to hang up spare gear. The city also bought us ten new sections of two-inch hose that we put on the fire engine. It's great when you start to see everything that you have worked hard for to finally come together. The eight of us had put in a lot of time and effort to get this department completed and functioning for the safety of the town as a whole.

As we were getting ready to go, Joe and Chief told us that on the first of the month, a man from the state would be coming out to install a pager system for us through the sheriff's department so they can tone out all of us at one time instead of calling each one of us at a time. We would be issued a radio also. "It's coming together, so have a good night, and see you all bright and early Saturday morning, here at the station."

I got a phone call about one thirty, Saturday morning, from Mrs. Mattie. "Todd, we have a fire at Florence Marina, the DNR lay-down yard. Can you respond?"

I told her, "Yes, I'm on my way." I got up, slipped my socks on, then grabbed my turnout pants and boots and pulled them up. Lisa woke up, and I told her, "What's up?" and I leaned down, kissed her, and told her I love her and where I was going. It didn't seem like much to say "I love you," but in what I do, it is every much important because, in any given day, it could be the last thing I said to her, and I would always want her to know how I felt about her. I grabbed my keys and flashlight and headed out the front door toward my truck.

The good thing about this morning is that it was dark. Why? Because on a dark night, the deer usually bed down and don't move around and cross the road. My Dodge Dakota is a deer magnet. I have already hit three deer and a pig—yes, a pig. I headed out of the driveway toward the canyons, which is west of my house, and it took me about ten minutes to reach the Marina.

The DNR has a lay-down yard across the street from the Marina, where they keep treated wood for the docks, boats, and materials to keep the park look good. As I turned off thirty-nine on to twenty-seven, I could see the large fire, and Chief and Greg were already here. I pulled my truck off the road back from the fire, got out, grabbed my jacket and helmet, and headed for the tanker.

Greg and I grabbed the portable dump tank off the tanker (or "red neck swimming pool" as we like to call it) and set it up in the driveway of the lay-down yard. Chief then backed the tanker up to it, and we filled it up. Then Chief headed to Omaha three miles away to fill the tanker back up. Mike came up in his truck and helped me set up, and we got our SCBAs as Greg was pulling the engine around to draft out of the dump tank, which held one thousand gallons of water, but that goes quick if you don't keep an eye on it.

Greg, Mike, and I walked down in front of the building. We saw that it was burning very well with all the paint and treated lumber. As we walked to where we were going to make our stand, we saw a fiberglass boat hull burning, so Greg told us to put our masks on, tuck the hose in our jackets for there were a lot of contaminants in the smoke that were very harmful, and save our tank air. After, he showed us where to set up, and then we went back to the engine, pulled off the two-inch line, dragged it back to the spot, and got ready.

Greg came over the radio, and we told him to charge the line as it was getting a little warm where we were. The line charged up, and we started to knock the flames down and got a handle on it. And all of a sudden, the water pressure drops, and Greg came over the radio. "We are out of water, but Chief is backing the tanker up to the dump tank, and I'll have you back up in a minute."

The flames that we had knocked back slowly started to creep back toward us, and let me tell you, it was a helpless feeling sitting there with no water, and the fire was coming back toward you. You'd think it was time to run.

And then Greg said, "Here it comes." Relief. Cool water. But it was short-lived as we keep running low on water again. We kept doing this until Greg told us to move down on the end and just keep it from penetrating the last wall. There was a big cabin cruiser sitting fifteen feet from the side of the building, and it couldn't be moved because it was dry-docked on wooden stands.

Mike and I moved to make our last stand at the side of the wall and held the water until the fire got to the wall. Then we kept it soaked and cool and prayed it wouldn't go beyond the wall, for if it does. .. well, the boat was expensive, full of fuel, and sat close to the woods. If it got through us, it will be a very long night.

We made our stand and held the fire back. An hour later, we had a wall standing and we had a boat, and the heat from the fire melted the plastic tarp that was over the boat. Talking about hot. We even had to go on air the last few minutes because it got very hot on us. Mike and I finished wetting the hot spots in the building and started to pull the hose back to the truck as the power company got here to pull the jack and cut the power to the building.

I looked at my watch, and it was three o'clock in the morning, and we have to be at the station in the morning at nine thirty for the fair on the square. This was going to be a long day, but fun. I got back to the house and slipped in the door, and as quite as I could, I took a shower and eased into bed. And just as I close my eyes, Lisa whispered, "Glad you're home." Then she rolled over, and we drifted back to sleep.

My alarm woke me up from a deep sleep, and it felt like I just closed my eyes two seconds ago. But it was eight o'clock and time to rise and shine. I had an hour and a half to get to the station, get everything set up, and cooked for the fair. I got dressed, and before I leave, I told Lisa to bring the kids to town later, do some looking around, and see if she can find something neat for the kids.

I got to the station, and Greg was inside the kitchen, talking to the EMTs that were working that day. They were Woody and Chad, the dynamic duo. I liked Woody and thought a lot of him. He knew his job and was very good at it. He was also the biggest movie buff I have ever met. He could tell you the name of the movie, who starred in it, and even what year it came out. He had a big collection of playStation games, something to keep him busy when he was on down time.

Greg and I started by pulling the tanker out of the bay and parked it around behind the station so we could set up the tables. The wives were going to be selling the one hundred T-shirts that we had for ten dollars each and the two hundred raffle tickets that we had for five dollars each. All the firemen were going to be selling the chicken fingers and french fries and meeting and getting to know the public. Rusty came in and had the chicken and potatoes, and we got set up and started to cook some chicken. The smell of the food drew a lot of people over to the new fire station. We also handed out some important phone numbers for medical emergencies, fires, and the sheriff department on a magnet to stick to your refrigerator for quick reference.

We met a lot of town people and council members, and a lot of people that, if not for this event, we would not meet. I took a break, got a drink, and sat down behind the fire engine for a couple of minutes. Then I heard a young boy and asked his mom if he could sit in the truck, and she said, "No, not today." I got up and walked over to where he was at. I knelt down, got eye-to-eye with him, and asked him if he would like to sit in the fire engine, and he said yes. So I opened the door and sit him up in the cab of the engine. He grabbed the steering wheel and to see him smile made me think, *That's why I do what I do.*

His mom was standing there, and she looked at me and said, "You just made his day." I also looked back at him and showed him how to turn the lights on, and he was speechless. I let him sit there a few more minutes, and then I helped him down. He ran over to his grandmother and told her what he got to do. His mom said, "Thank you," and then they walked back across the street.

Then I saw Lisa carrying Ryan and Dustin standing beside her, and that made my day, except maybe a little more sleep, but I'd just get in bed a little early tonight. Or maybe not. Lisa and the kids came in the station. I picked Dustin up and sat him in the fire truck, and he just smiled. I introduced Lisa to some of the other wives, and they talked as we guys finished cleaning up the station.

We sold out of all the T-shirts and raffle tickets, and Joe said we need to print some more T-shirts for the raffle drawing next month, and I agreed with him. Afterward, we head to the house for some relaxation, I hope.

On Monday morning at work, Billy and I were running some conduit under the paper machine for a pump motor. Billy is my tool buddy; we have worked together for at least ten years. He is like a younger brother, good worker, and cuts up a lot, and that is why I like working with him. plus he has always been a friend and helped me when I needed it.

I started talking to him about the weekend and how we had raised a lot of money for the fire department. He said he would buy two raffle tickets and the other guys would probably buy some too. Billy said, "Five dollars for a chance at a three-hundred-dollar shotgun." The mill guys might even buy some of them.

I ended up selling seventy tickets at the mill for a chance at the shotgun alone, and they didn't even want a chicken dinner. Dwight and John, our supervisors, even bought two each. Dwight even told me to ask some of the contractors to donate some money or tools that we will need, like ladders or some hand tools. They could write those off on their taxes as a donation. The union contractors donated four hundred dollars, and one volunteered to donate a concrete saw. It was used but it was a fifteen-hundred-dollar tool. *Wow.*

I even sold some T-shirts to some of the guys I worked with, and they commented on how much they liked the T-shirts. I had a great day for the department and went home feeling very good about it.

TRAINING TIME

AS IN EVERY fire department, training is a constant job because the more you do something, the better you get at it. And you also learn from mistakes you make along the way. All the training can also lead to easier ways to do some tasks the second time around. That is what we call "tricks of the trade" or "second nature."

It was sometime in November, a Saturday morning, and it was getting cold. Frost was on the ground and a lot of trees had lost most of their leaves when Chief informed us that he had gotten permission for some training. Chief had gotten permission from Robert Edison to burn an old plantation house that was on his property out US thirty-nine. So he planned for us to go out, do some training techniques (like making entry from different locations), and observe how fire spreads in a house and how long it takes to get out before it is too late. Whenever we got a chance to train on an actual house and do a live burn, it helped us very much. The live burns put you right there in the middle of real situations that, if done wrong, could actually hurt or kill you. Chief even told me that you would see people react differently when it's for real.

Dan, Rusty, Matt, chief and I arrived about seven thirty. Chief backed the tanker up in front of the house so we could start setting the dump tank up. The dump tank is an important piece of equipment to a rural county fire department like ours. It could also mean the difference between putting the fire out, and losing control of the situation at hand. Dan then took the tanker back to town to refill it.

As Dan was pulling out of the driveway, Joe and Mike pulled up with the engine and pulled around in front of the house, but not too close, so we could set it up to draft out of the dump tank. Chief then walked us around the house and showed us how he had covered the windows with plywood to make it like a real house inside and keep the smoke in to get the full effect of what we would face on a real call. Everyone went back to their vehicles and got their turnout gear and self-contained breathing apparatuses and brought it all up to the front of the house, and we waited for Dan to get back.

Chief told us that he had invited a couple of firemen from Georgetown, which is a small town a few miles down the road from us. He said it was good to know firemen from around the county and train together just in case we need some help in the middle of the night. We were not total strangers.

After Dan got back with the tanker truck and the other firemen arrived, Chief walked us all around the house to show us how he wanted to do the training so everyone would be on the same page. He also said we would each have a partner, enter two at a time to put the fire out, and then back out the same way we went in. I lucked out—I got Rusty as my partner, and he said I could be the nozzle man, and he had my back. I couldn't lie that I was a little nervous as this would be my first entry into a burning structure, and you'd never know what to expect.

Once we got our gear on and were at the front of the house, Chief and Joe gave us a few more safety tips to remember once inside the house. "One, if you hear the siren from the engine, pull out immediately with no hesitation," Joe said. "Two, never leave your partner. And three, if you see anything that might be a problem, point it out to me or Chief right then, and be safe."

I put my helmet on and fastened the chin strap. Rusty helped me get my hood tucked in and my collar closed to keep the heat off my skin. I also checked him, and we then had to wait for Mike and Dan to get suited up also. They would be the backup team just in case something went wrong; they can come in and help get us out.

I was a little nervous as I got on my knees to enter the house. I took a few deep breaths to make sure my SCBA was working and I had the nozzle in my hands. And all of a sudden, I heard a big roar inside the house as Joe ignited the fire, and then Chief slapped me on the helmet to go.

I started to crawl across the floor in such a fast pace that I had left Rusty, and he told me to slow down because I was going too fast. I stopped and waited for Rusty to catch up, and all at once, a big rat, as big as a small dog, came running at me. It scared the shit out of me, so I opened up the nozzle to scare it off, and it ran around me. I turned and followed it with a straight stream of water, and it ran right past Rusty. And yes, I soaked him good before I could turn the nozzle off.

"Stop!" was all I had to hear.

"I'm sorry," I said, "but did you see the size of that rat?" "No" was all Rusty said because all he saw was water.

I laughed for a couple of seconds, and then we moved on ahead. The smoke was starting to get thick in the house, and it was coming down from the ceiling and making it hard to see. I had to start feeling for the walls as we got farther inside the house to keep a sense of moving in one direction. Then when we reached the fire. It was easier to see and a pretty neat sight to see. No, I'm not a pyromaniac, but it is something to behold, and good to know how it moves around the room.

I stopped to watch the thermal layering that happened as a fire burned and turned the material into a gaseous state, and the smoke goes up to the ceiling. As the fire continued to burn, the room would become so hot that all the gases that were coming off the objects in the room would reach their flash point and ignite. Flash point is the temperature at which each gas will catch on fire. Almost at once, the flames will then flashover the room, causing a flash over, and that is what will trap you in the house.

So we watched the fire, and as it got to the point of flashover, we put it out. A big red ball of flame jumped at me, and I opened up the nozzle and shot a straight stream of water on the fire, and all of a sudden, the steam and ashes hit me in the face mask and almost knocked me down. I guess that was the reasoning behind getting down on your knees and staying low.

I cut it off after hitting it a couple more times with some straight streams of water and cut the nozzle off. I listened for the crackling sound that the instructor in the state class told us to do. When I didn't hear any sound, I move closer to where the fire was at. I had put it out, so Rusty and I backed out of the house to let the next team come in.

We crawled back to the front door, and chief told us, "Good job" as we walked out of the house.

Rusty shook my hand and said, "Good job, Todd."

We walked over to the engine and took our SCBAs and turnout jackets off so we could cool down and get something to drink. I never knew that the thick gear on, the thirty pound SCBA, the ten-pound helmet, and the boots would wear you out so quickly, but they did.

We sat down and started talking about our jobs and careers, family, and other things on our minds, and about halfway through one of my stories, I thought about what I had heard about male bonding. That happens when you get to know some of your male friends, and they get to know you as far as knowing your wife, kids, what kind of work you do, and just all about you in general. That's when it hit me. If I have to go in to a burning house one night, these guys would know what I have to lose, and I would know what they have to lose, and that was what bonds us together as brothers.

Matt, Mike, Joe: they all have families that I have meet and known and they have meet mine, so we all know what each other puts on the line every time we respond to a call.

A couple of weeks later, we got the chance again to burn another house. Some of the land owners had a lot of property with old abandoned houses on them that were rotting down. They wanted the land for planting crops, so this gave us a good chance to practice on a real house and to get more familiar with doing it for real.

This particular Saturday, I got to the house on US thirty-nine, about the same time as Dan did. We parked across the street from the house as not to be in the way. We would find out later that we should have parked farther up the road. Chief arrived around seven thirty, pulled the fire engine in the driveway, and parked about fifty feet from the side of the house. Rusty and Mike arrived after Chief and parked behind Dan. We all grabbed our turnout gear, brought it over, and put it on the front porch of the house while we took a look around the house.

Rusty and I walked around the outside of the house to check and see what kind of bushes and debris was against it. We found a few bushes, but the biggest thing was a huge magnolia tree right beside the front porch.

Mike and Chief went in the front door, and two steps in, Mike's foot went through the floor, so they came back outside. We looked in the windows, and there was nothing inside to cause any problems. Chief made the decision to just burn it down and keep it from spreading because it would be too dangerous to do any training inside. Mike and Chief sprayed some gas inside the house to help start the fire as Rusty, Dan, and I set the engine up and pulled away from the house. I pulled about fifty feet of inch-and-a-half hose off and around the back of the house to keep an eye on the back side. The wind was calm, and I wet the grass around the back and up the side of the house.

Chief ignited the gas and closed the door behind him as he came out. Rusty was on the front corner of the house with an inch-and-a-half hose ready just in case. Mike and Chief put a time on the house to see how long it would take to totally engulf the house. At two minutes, the very thick smoke was coming out the roof vents, and at two and a half minutes, the house was totally engulfed. If you were not out of that house at two and a half minutes, you would have been a fatality or DRT (dead right there). I have always heard how fire is like a living, breathing animal, and that day, I saw it with my own eyes.

As the house started to burn and the fire spread throughout the house, it became an inferno, and it got hotter and hotter. Standing there, I could feel the wind being sucked into the house from where I was at. I was a little worried about the magnolia tree at the front of the house because, as the wind picked up, it could blow embers around when it catches on fire. I didn't have long to wait, and it sounded like a jet taking off. It was loud and scary as it burned.

We kept watching the house, and as I looked across the street where our vehicles were, I thought I saw some flames or a reflection on the wind shields. Then Dan yelled that there was a fire behind my truck. I looked again, and the fires were higher than the front of my truck. That's when Mike yelled, spotted fires, and ran over to the vehicles with a shovel in his hands. I gave Chief my nozzle and headed that way too. Mike and I started to stomp the fire out with our boots, and I grabbed a shovel off my truck, and as we were stomping the fire out, we looked like we were in a fire ant bed. I even got some embers in my hair, and I was swatting my head and stomping the grass. It was crazy.

The woods were on fire too, and we ran in and out of the trees, and it felt like we were in a firestorm. I felt rain, but it was only Rusty spraying the woods from the engine with a hose, and we finally got it out. The house was on the ground by the time Mike and I came out of the woods. We looked like a bunch of coal miners. Rusty hosed us down, and it felt great. As Mike and I sat on the tailboard of the fire truck, all wet and beat, Greg and Joe pulled up and asked if we were OK. We just looked at each other and said yeah.

Chief and Rusty finished wetting the house down. We made sure it was completely out and then loaded the hose on the truck and headed back to town. We cleaned the truck and hose and put everything back in place for the next call. I left the station that day with a better understanding of teamwork and how fast a situation could turn in to a struggle for life or death.

Well, August was coming in, and Chief and Joe told us at the meeting that we were going to have a state training officer to come in and do some BLEVE training out at the high school. The training would consist of one eight-hour day of films, question-and-answer, and a fifty-question test and an eight-hour hands-on fire training of a simulation propane tank.

I had seen the results of a boiling liquid expanding vapor explosion on TV, and in every conclusion, it leveled everything around it and, in some cases, killed some good firemen that where in the wrong place at the wrong time. The class was on a Saturday and Sunday at the end of the month, and everyone showed up on time except Chief. He overslept, or at least that was his story, and he stuck to it. I arrived at seven thirty along with Rusty and Matt. Mike and Greg were already there since they had worked last night on the ambulance. The state guy got there around eight, and class began on time.

The training officer started off by asking if anybody knew the definition of BLEVE, and a couple of us did, so he told the rest of us the proper definition, which is "an explosion caused by the rupture of a vessel containing a pressurized liquid above its boiling point. He also told us that the best sound you can hear is the loud roar of the release valve, and it will scare you to death when you hear it. But if you don't hear it, that is bad because if it cannot vent the pressure, it will explode. And you do not want to be around when it does.

"Got it," we all agreed.

BLEVEs can result from a lot of different causes like mechanical failure to a propane tank, derailment of a train, or a simple traffic accident. When a BLEVE occurs, it can scatter debris for hundreds of feet with tremendous force, releasing the content of the tank, which can ignite, causing even more damage and fatalities.

We all took notes and asked questions and the state guy told us that we should know the basic properties of lp (liquified petroleum) gas, and this would allow us to make proper decisions regarding exposure and how to evacuate the occupants of a house or vehicle. We all took the test and headed to lunch for a break in the day and to give the teacher time enough to check our test and let us know how much we didn't know.

After lunch I learned that I missed a couple because I read too much the question. It was often the simplest answer to the most difficult question that is right. But we all passed, and I knew we would. After we checked our test scores, the teacher told us about what to expect tomorrow, to get plenty of rest, and to meet back here in the morning at ten.

On Sunday morning, we all got to the station around nine thirty. Even Chief was early. We liked to pick on Ray, but he can dish it out as well as he can take it. The class started on time, and the teacher jumped right back in where we left off with a film about one of the worst BLEVEs in US history. In 1995, the Kansas City Fire Department responded to a twenty-five-thousand-gallon gas tank fire that exploded and killed five firefighters, the largest loss of life in the Kansas City Fire Department history. He told us that, by being firemen, our first instinct is to control the fire or leaking gas, but we should take into consideration and weigh the risks over the benefits. In some cases, the best course of action may be to retreat to a safer area and monitor the fire from a safe distance; this way, the public and fire personnel are out of any danger. The teacher said in concluding the class that he was there to warn us of the potential dangers of a BLEVE and train us so we didn't have any similar incidents like the one in Kansas City. The teacher told us to go to lunch, get our gear, and meet him at the high school in one hour.

We arrived at the school, and the state teacher had set up a propane truck over to one side of the parking lot and had ran a gas line over to a mock propane tank in the center of the parking lot for us to practice on. Chief pulled the engine about a hundred feet from the mock propane tank, and we laid out two inch-and- a-half lines from the engine. The objective was to shield ourselves from the fire as the three firemen would approach the fire with the nozzle on fog spray like a wall of water, the two firemen with the nozzles would open up, and the middle fireman would reach in and cut the valve off as we get to the tank.

We all suited up, and Rusty, Mike, and I got to go first. I grabbed a hose, and Rusty got another, and Mike was the middle man. The tank was lit. We put our SCBAs on and charge the lines. The teacher gave us the go-ahead, and Rusty and I opened our nozzles to a fog spray and got side by side as to keep the water together and from the ground as not to let the flames come under and burn us we slowly walk toward the tank. We got about ten feet from the tank, and the pop-off valve goes off. And let me tell you, your butt would tighten up, and it was a scary sound to hear, but like the teacher said, "it is a good sound to hear also."

We stopped, and Rusty turned just enough for Mike to reach his hand out and turn the valve to cut it off. Then we retraced our steps, and when we were far enough back from the tank, we cut the nozzles off, took our masks off, cut our air tanks off, and just smiled for that was mission complete.

After the rest of the guys completed their time, we loaded up the hose, headed back to town to finish up the class, hanged the hose to dry, and got the engine ready for our next call. The teacher told us in closing that we did a good job and if we need his assistance for anything, we shouldn't hesitate to call the state office,

"Thanks for lunch," he added.

TEAMWORK

WELL, IT WAS getting close to Christmas or, as we like to call it "the silly season," and some people can do some crazy things. It was December 14, and being an electrician, I know that when you plug up a Christmas tree, you first make sure to keep the tree watered so it doesn't dry out. And then you don't put too many lights on it as not to short the circuit out. I don't know if people just don't think it could happen to them or they are just immune to the laws of physics. Well, let me tell you that the reality of it is that we all are not strangers to those things happening to us, and that was what happened around two thirty that morning.

We had all been issued our pagers, and if we thought they didn't work, we found out that they did, and they are loud the first time they went off for real.

Mrs. Mattie came over the pager, and it scared me almost to death. "Lumpkin firemen, we have a fire on Elm Street, time out two thirty."

I got up, put my turnout pants and boots on, and pulled the suspenders over my shoulders as I walked to the living room. I grabbed my keys and radio from the table and headed out the door toward my truck. I could probably sleep on the way to town since I have drove it so much it is burned in my mind. But it was also a clear night, and the moon was out, so I have to be alert for deer, and I sure didn't want to end up in a ditch.

As I rolled up on the scene, I saw Stanley standing by the road. He was not in uniform, so I got my gear on and headed toward the engine where he was standing. Stanley is a deputy sheriff, and he is tall and big as a bear, but when he gets to know you, he is a great guy and fun to be around.

I asked him what was up. He looked at me, and he was crying. And he told me that this was his mom and dad's house. I hurried over to the engine and checked in with Chief, and he sent me to the front of the house where Greg was, and when I got there, we put our masks on and headed in the house.

It was a shotgun house, so we headed down the hall toward the kitchen in the back of the house. I took the lead, and Greg followed me in with the hose. I got close to the kitchen, and something hit so hard that I fell to my side and told Greg to *stop*. I felt like I was a fish out of water, flopping around, and I couldn't think of why this was happening. Greg grabbed me by the boots and told me to drop the hose. Then he pulled me back to him, and we both crawled back out of the house.

Greg looked at me and asked me if I was OK. And I said, "Yes, but I know what the problem was."

"What?" Greg said, and I just walked around to the side of the house and pulled the meter out of the meter socket to cut power to the house off.

I walked back around to the front of the house, and as Chief walked up, I handed him the meter as he asked, "What's the problem?"

Greg and I just looked at him then we headed back into the house. I crawled back down the hall, and most of the fire was in the bathroom and kitchen areas. I got the fire under control. Then I hear a hissing sound, so I asked Greg, "Do you hear that sound?"

And he said, "Yes, it is coming from the bathroom."

I turned and crawled over to the door, and when I opened it up, the lid for the tank on the toilet was off, and water was shooting straight up to the ceiling, almost like a sprinkler head. I told Greg, and we got a laugh out of it.

After the fire was out and had ventilated and done our salvage overhaul of the house, Greg and I went back down the hallway to see what was going on. I raised up the carpet and found an extension cord running under the carpet for the Christmas tree, the TV, and the VCR. It was frayed, so it was shocking me since I had the hose and was wet from the water with my hand touching it.

Electricity and water don't mix too well, and I just looked at Greg and said, "Thanks for watching out for me. That could have been bad." That is why we go in together to watch each other's back. It is something that every fireman should remember.

I walked over to the engine, changed out my SCBA tank, and put it back in my truck. Before I left, I walk over to where Stanley was standing and asked him how his mom and dad were doing. He said they were shaken but still here.

I told him, "That's good, and if you need anything, just holler. See you around, big guy." I went, got in my truck, headed for home, and just thanked the lord they are OK because, as long as they are alive, things would get better.

In our next meeting, we all felt like it was Christmas day. A salesman from Firefox was there to measure us for our new fire suits. The ones were made from Komaxx. We picked out MSA (Mine Safety Appliances) helmets and ranger boots, and he also gave us hoods and gloves. He said we should have them in a couple of weeks and pick out a truck and design it so we could get started on building it.

I enjoyed all the testing and learning new skills to make our department better equipped to handle any kind of situation that may arise in the future. Our department has been trained in hazmat (hazardous material) for first responders; vehicle extrication; and street survival (one, two, and three) for rescue specialist. And I'm now an emergency medical technician and so are some of the other firemen in our town.

The training is what keeps you up on the latest techniques because everything keeps changing. Take for instance the way a house is built—it is more energy efficient that it is insulated to keep the cold in and the hot out. It also creates a vacuum inside that, if you have a fire inside your house and you are asleep, the fire will use up all the oxygen in the house, and you go into a deep sleep and don't wake up. Some of the new cars that are on the road have engines that are made of different kinds of metals that, if they catch on fire and we try to put them out with water, they explode. So we have to continue to train and keep up with all the new material that is being trucked on the roads today. For instance, if a semitruck wrecks and it spills hazardous material, it could kill a lot of people.

The city council and the community had worked with us so well that we were anticipating the new fire engine in a couple of months. The only thing I would like was to pick up some new recruits to help us out.

Sometimes we get help when we don't need it, and if bull in a china shop means anything to you, that's what it is like when someone tries to help but doesn't know the first thing about safety or how to attack a fire.

We had just one of those close encounters one afternoon a couple of weeks later. I was helping my brother in his antique shop on the square when we got the call that a house two blocks from us was on fire. I got in my truck and drove to the house that was smoking a lot when I reached it. Chief and Greg had already arrived, so I pulled around behind the house and got my gear on. Matt arrived shortly after and told me to set up at the back door, but not to breach it, and not to let anyone come in there until he gave the word. I set up at the back door as Chief and Greg goes in the front.

A lot of people started to gather around and wanted to help, and I just told them we have it and to stand back across the street, but they just kept coming back. Then one guy came up and wanted to bust out the back door glass, and I told him to get back now.

That's when big Stanley pulled up in his squad car, and I asked him to keep these people back. Stanley turned to the crowd and said, "Get back, and I don't want to tell you twice or someone will be going to jail, so get back."

"Thanks, Stanley," I said, and we put the fire out.

It was because of a mattress and a cigarette that someone had left for some reason, but no one was in the house. The family was on vacation. Odd, I know, but everything turned out OK.

After the fire, I told Matt what had happened, and I found out that, at a fire scene, the fire department outranks anybody, even the police or sheriff's department. And if there had been an actual fire and a door was open, it could cause a draft in the house, just like a chimney effect, and get somebody hurt or killed. If the right circumstances occurred, even a back draft or flashover would kill a lot of firemen each year, the guys that get paid for doing this job.

Matt and I got to clean up the fire scene, which is part of the duties of a fireman. people think all we do is just come out, put water on the fire, make a mess, and then get our toys up and leave. I'm here to tell you that when the smoke settles, we go in the house and set up fans to draft the smoke out so we can do salvage and overhaul. This consists of pulling out any cloths or furniture that might reignite after we have left the scene or removing water the best we can so the fire inspector can get inside and find out the cause of the fire. I have even seen the fire inspectors come out with dogs to sniff out any accelerant that might have been used in starting fires.

After we finished cleaning up the mess, we walked over to where Greg was standing, and he said he had something for us. He handed us our very own pASS device.

I looked at Matt and said, "All right. What is it?"

Matt said, "It is a personal alert safety system. If you go down for any reason in a fire and stop moving for about twenty-five seconds, it will go off so we can find you and get you out before it's too late. Got it?" Matt told me that even a simple fire could turn deadly if you forgot the small things, so I should make sure that I activated it before each fire.

Greg then looked at me and said, "Come to the station so I can give you your new turnout gear."

And that was a good day, especially when I put it on for the first time. I felt like I was. .. well, I just felt good and proud to be a part of something like this with a bunch of guys that I enjoy being around.

GRASS CREEK AND THE OMAHA CALLS

SOMETIMES WE GO for two maybe three weeks before we have a fire, which is fine by me because, as long as you don't have a fire, that means people get what we are telling them. But sometimes they don't.

It was a Saturday, and all I had planned was cleaning up the yard with my two boys and watching the Auburn-Florida game tonight. I'm a big SEC fan. I woke up around nine, in which it is nice to sleep in for a change, and helped Lisa cook breakfast: grits, eggs, and sausages and toast. We ate breakfast and headed outside to enjoy the sunshine and being together and doing some manly stuff. Dustin was seven, and he was learning to ride his bicycle and play baseball. I hope he learns to love baseball like I did because that was the one thing that my dad and I have in common.

I remember growing up, and he taught me that baseball is a lot like life. You have to work not only as a part of a team, but you also have to excel as an individual. I guess that is also true about firefighting. The better the team, the better the department, and you take care of your teammates.

I had to have a break, and I sit down to cool off. Dustin came over to check on me. We started talking about baseball and guy stuff—you know, bugs, girls—and he sneaked in that he wanted a big toy Tonka truck and asked about my leg where I have scars from the burns I got when I was young. And as we talked, I realized that just listening to him is very important even if you don't agree with what a kid says. Just listening can strengthen the bond between you and your kids, and in my line of work, that may be all he remembers if I'm not here. We got the yard work done around five, and we got baths and ready for the night.

Lisa had fixed supper, and she cooks like my mom, but that's not why I married her. I met Lisa because one of her friends was head over heels in love with my cousin Sid. Her car was in the shop, so Lisa had to bring her over to our apartment where Sid and I lived. I think it was lust she was feeling, but it turned out to be fate for Lisa and me. Lisa is my high school sweetheart and my true love. That happens only once in a lifetime. We dated for fifteen months because she still had to graduate from high school before we could take the plunge. In that time, I found out that Lisa's mom went to high school with my mom and uncle, and her Granddaddy Moore knew my granddad that had passed away before I was born.

When we had our rehearsal dinner, it was like a family reunion. My mom came over and hugged Grandddaddy Moore, and she told him, "Do you remember me?"

And Grandddaddy Moore said, "like it was yesterday."

Lisa's Granddaddy Moore told me stories about my granddad and helped me know just what kind of man he was. He even told me some great stories about the first time meeting him at a gas station in their Model Ts. It was great. I still remember meeting new family members at the wedding, and it has been fourteen years ago. I even found out when I meet Matt that he and his wife, Ann, got married the same day as Lisa and I did, except they got married at 7:00 p.m., and we got married at 2:00 p.m.

After supper we got ready for the big game and played around a little in the house and put all the toys away right up when it started. Everything was as it was every time we played Alabama. You're on the edge of your seat. Anticipation and nerves keep you coming back to watch. I had put Dustin and Ryan to bed around half time as they were getting sleepy, and Lisa and I continued to watch and pull for our team, the Auburn Tigers, and Coach Terry Bowden to pull it out at the last minute.

I was getting ready for a great last minute field goal, and the pager went off. "Lumpkin firemen, we have a possible drowning at Grass Creek on US thirty- nine, time out ten fifteen."

I got up, went in the bedroom, changed into my turnout boots, and pants and came back in the living room. I kissed Lisa and told her, "let me know who wins. I love you and will see you in a little while." We always say that because I never want to say good-bye that is kind of a negative tone. That's not what I want to convey to her because I always plan on coming back in one piece.

I jumped in the truck and headed toward Florence Marina, which is on the Chattahoochee River. The word *Chattahoochee* is an Indian word meaning "treacherous water," and that was why my parents always told us to not go around it for it has killed a lot of people over the years.

I turned on my DVD player and started listening to AC/DC's "Who Made Who," and it calmed the butterflies down in me as I drive to the marina. As I approach thirty-nine, Dan, in the rescue truck with the boat that we got about three weeks ago donated by the Sanger family that owned the gas station in town, flew by in front of me followed by Rusty and Matt. I fell in line behind them, and as I took off, Mike came up behind me as we headed toward the river.

I looked down, and I was doing seventy-five miles an hour, and the marina came up pretty quick. We turned right on thirty-nine, and it was about a mile up the road to the bridge, and the inlet called Grass Creek is just beyond it. Dan pulled to the side of the road, and Mike and I pulled off on a dirt road that leads down to the creek. We jumped out, left our lights on so we could back Dan in, and got everything set up to search for the survivors or bodies as quick as we could.

It was dark, and the water was calm and smooth as glass and very cold as Mike and I walked up to the edge of it. It was very quiet and eerie as we looked and listened for any signs of life, but all we saw was the content of the boat floating on top of the water. I went back to the rescue truck and got a pike pole twelve feet long out and walked back over to the edge.

The first thing I pulled out of the water was a life preserver and then another one. Dan told me and Mike to guide him as he backed the boat up to the water so we could get it in and hopefully find the bodies before they were lost. Mike and Rusty went out in the boat and started to feel for anything under the water with the two aluminum poles that are twelve feet long. They just paddled around as not to disturb the water just in case we'd see any air bubbles or hear any sounds that might help. Dan came over to where I was at, and he told me, "The three guys were going to night fish like they had done many times before. They pushed off from the bank and as they were getting situated, one of them stood up, and when the boat rocked to the side, he went to grab the plastic seat, and it broke. He fell in and tipped the boat over.

"The man that called us said he swam for the shore, not knowing that the other two guys could not swim. When he got to the shore, he turned around and tried to help the others, but in the cold and darkness, they were already gone. Then he ran to a house down the road and called the sheriff's department. I have called the state dive team, and they are en route, but it will take about two hours for them to get here.

"Meanwhile, we'll keep searching until they arrive. I'm going to let you and Matt go back home since we are short on man power. Get some rest and call the sheriff's department at six in the morning to see if we need you back down here. Hopefully, we will find them, but in conditions like this, it is a crap shoot at best. It's 1:00 a.m. now, so go get some sleep for it is going to be a long night. Talk to you in the morning.

I walked over to my truck, got in, and cranked it up. I turned on the heat and waited a minute for it to blow some warm air on me. I couldn't imagine what these two men must have felt. I'd like to be able to tell them to put your life jacket on. It only takes a minute, but it will save your family from a lifetime without you and the grieving. If only I could tell them. But I can't.

I got home about one thirty, and Lisa had left me a note on the table that read, "War eagle, we won 18-17, love you." I know that's a good thing, and any other time, I'd be celebrating. But now just didn't seem like the time. I sat down at the table in the kitchen and thought about the day, and winding down, I said a prayer for the two men's families, set my clock, and got in bed.

I woke up at five thirty and called the sheriff's department to check the status on the scene. John told me that the bodies were recovered around two thirty. I hung up the phone and thanked God that they were recovered.

I enjoy the feeling of helping people that are appreciative of the effort from you, but sometimes, you meet the one that doesn't appreciate anything you do for them.

It takes a lot to stay calm when your adrenaline is pumping through you. It was on a Tuesday morning, about five o'clock, when we got the call to head to Omaha. It is a small town of about two hundred people, about eighteen miles from Lumpkin, and it sets on the Chattahoochee River.

They had a volunteer fire department in the past, and through the years, it has been hard to find people willing to form a fire department and get someone to run it. If you go around the country you will find that a lot of volunteer departments have the same trouble: no one wants to donate the time and effort until you have a fire. Then everyone wants to help till the fire goes out. Then it goes back to don't have the time or not interested.

We have the same problem in Lumpkin. No one thinks it will ever happen to them, but when it does, then they find fault with how it was handled, or "What took you so long to get to my house?" This is what happened on the morning.

I'm awakened by the pager, and Mrs. Mattie said, "Lumpkin firemen, we have a house fire in Omaha, time out five o'clock."

I got out of bed, slipped my boots on, pulled the suspenders on my turnout pants up over my shoulders, and slipped out of the bedroom. I grabbed my keys and radio off the corner table and headed out the door.

I radioed Mrs. Mattie that I'm en route as I headed to my black Dodge Dakota. Lisa let me trade in my old truck for my new Dodge Dakota this past weekend. Mike and I put some red and white wigwag lights in the front headlight for, when I go on a fire call, I can let people know I'm en route to a fire.

I cranked up and pulled out of the driveway and turn them on. *Wow they look fantastic,* I thought. I turned on my CD player with AC/DC's "Who Made Who" and headed toward Omaha. I crossed US twenty-seven and headed toward thirty-nine that runs in front of providence Canyon. This is the back way so I didn't have to go through town, and it saves some time also.

The moon was still out this morning, and it made it a little easier to see as I headed down the hill from the canyon. I picked up a little speed as I approached a three-mile straightaway in front of the old Bradley hog pens and cornfield. I was driving eighty miles an hour as I look down to check my speedometer.

Chief came over the radio and asked what my location was. I picked up the radio and told him where I'm at, and he told me he was turning off thirty-nine into Omaha.

I said, "Copy. I'm about two miles from Florence Marina." I turned to put the radio in the seat, and when I looked back to the road, a doe deer ran in front of me. I lifted my foot off the gas pedal to slow down because there was usually something behind her like a buck or yearling. The doe made it across, and I hold my breath. And then all of a sudden, a buck slammed into the door of my truck so hard that, at eighty miles an hour, he pushed me off the road and into the ditch.

I held on to the steering wheel, tapped the brakes as not to lock the tires up, and made the truck flip over and really messed it up. I finally stopped, undid my seat belt, and got out of the truck. I looked at the damage on my new truck, and I knew Lisa was going to kill me. The door was pushed in, and so was the quarter panel behind the back tire. I walked back up the road a little ways to see if I killed the deer or hurt it, but I saw nothing in the road or on the side of it.

I got back in my truck, and as I pulled out of the ditch on to the road, I saw that fifty feet farther down the ditch was a drain pipe for a driveway. If I had stayed in the ditch for fifty more feet, I would have hit the drainage pipe and really messed the truck up and possibly me too.

As I approached Omaha, I saw the fire just off thirty-nine about a block, so I pulled up in front of the pumper and got out, put my turnout jacket on, grabbed my helmet and SCBA, and headed toward the house where chief was standing in the front yard.

The house was smoking really bad, and as I put on my SCBA, Chief tells me not to bother because somebody has already knocked out all the windows. Chief told me to pull a inch-and-a-half hose line off the truck and moved around on the east side of the house to see if I can see the flames and put it out from there. I went and got the hose, and as I pulled it around to the side of the house, an old man yelled at me to move my ass and hurry up because his house was on fire. He made a few other smart-assed remarks. Then Chief came around there and told him to shut up, and he smarted off at chief too.

Chief turned away from him, came over to me, and told me, if he makes another comment, to just swing the water in his direction and soak him. I gave him a nod, and I moved toward the window, leaned in, and put the fire out. There was mostly smoke damage as we start to overhaul the house.

The man came up as we started to pull the hoses from the house, got in our faces, and demanded an answer for why it took so long for us to get here and to put the fire out. Chief came over and tells him how far we had to come and then asked him why he was not part of the volunteer department here in Omaha. And all he said was that he worked during the day and didn't have time to help.

I then told him, "I work over at the mill during the day, and on top of that, I just messed up a twenty-thousand-dollar truck trying to get here to make sure you and your family are safe. I don't understand why you are acting like we did not try hard enough because whoever knocked all the windows out, that's the person that burnt your house up."

He looked at me and Chief and said, "I did."

And all I said was "Well, sir, all I can say is that I'm sorry for your family." And then I helped Chief load the truck and I headed off to work.

I arrived at work about two hours late and went in the office to check in.

Dwight looked at me and said, "Hard morning?"

"Yes, I hit a buck on the way to a fire," I said. "Sorry I'm late."

And he just asked me, "How big was the buck? I wish we had a lot more people like you in this world, so go to work."

I'm a lucky guy to have friends like Dwight. He is truly one of a kind, and I know his dad, and he's the same way.

ONE OF OUR OWN

I ENJOY WHAT I do, and I love my life, and after all, I have a great wife and kids and family in general. I believe that in life, as in sports, that if you surround yourself with good friends and good people, your life will be happy. I have met a lot of nice people in Lumpkin since I've moved here two years ago.

I finally met Mrs. Mattie one day when I had to go and ask Matt something about county business. She is as nice in person as you would think she'd be since I had only heard her on the radio. If I meet someone, and they are nice and polite, I never forget that, and it makes you a friend to me.

It was a Friday morning around four thirty, and I had got up to take care of some business, and I figured I'd check on Ryan to see how he was feeling. He had been coughing and had a temperature before we put him to bed around ten o'clock. I looked inside the bedroom and felt his chest to make sure he was breathing and to pull the sheet back up over him so he wouldn't get any worse. I also looked in on Dustin and headed back to bed when the pager went off.

It was a male voice that I had never heard on the radio. "Richland firemen, we have a fire on Grady Street." Richland is about eight miles east of Lumpkin, and we back them up sometimes if needed. I stepped in to my boots, pulled my turnout pants up, and walked toward the front door. I waited a minute to see if we would be dispatched out for back up. And again I heard, "Richland firemen. .. " I grabbed my radio and keys and headed out the door.

I talked to Chief the other day, and he had mentioned that Richland had just got a bunch of new recruits. That might mean that we would be called to help handle some fire calls until they got some seasoning and real-life training under their belts. I radioed to dispatch halfway to town to see if they had responded yet, and John, the night dispatcher that fills in when Mrs. Mattie is off, said he had not reached anyone yet and that it was Mrs. Mattie's house that was called in. A weird feeling came over me when he told me that and I just pushed the pedal down a little farther so I could get there a little quicker.

Fifteen miles just seems so long when you have all these emotions running through you. I hope she got out and that someone else was a little closer. I crossed the four-lane interstate then headed into Richland, and down the road, I could see red and blue lights flashing, and I knew that somebody was there on the scene. I pulled around the fire truck and into the driveway of Mrs. Mattie's single wide trailer. I got out of my truck and saw that there was no fire, just a little smoke coming out of the front door a little.

I walked inside the house and Chief was inside looking around the living room to make sure the fire was out. We pulled a couch out from the wall and saw an extension cord for a light over a table plugged in to a receptacle, and it was smoking. I went to the electrical panel and cut off the main breaker to the house, and Chief and I removed the receptacle. I went to my truck and brought some wire caps back to place on the wires for safety. We finished checking the house out before I turned the power back on so we could use the exhaust fans to clean the smoke out of the house.

When I got through dealing with the house, I walked out back to Mike's squad car where Mrs. Mattie was sitting in the front seat with a blanket wrapped around her. I leaned down and gave her a hug, and she said, "Hey, Todd, how are you doing?"

And I just gave her a hug and said, "I'm glad you are OK." She said she was.

We planned on having a party once a year to get together as a team and with our families, and just have one special night together and get acquainted. Also on this night, we would give out promotions and thank each other for a job well done. I arrived around six thirty at Snooky's with Lisa and the boys, and we went in to the banquet room for our party.

Chief, his wife (Elizabeth), and Joe where already there, so was Matt, his wife (Ann), and their three kids, and we shook hands as I introduced Lisa, Dustin, and Ryan to them. We sat down at a table in the corner.

Everyone else arrived on time: Mike and his family; and Rusty, Angel, and little Russ; and Greg and his wife, Carol. I had never been to a gathering like this before, but I liked the fact that we were getting together to thank each other and meet our families. We were also going to move up in rank. Mike and I were hopefully going to be firemen now and not probies (probationary firemen).

We ate, talked, and had a great time getting to know everyone. Finally, Greg got up to speak for Chief, and he started telling us that we have come a long way in the past year.

I remember the old city barn and all the turnout gear that we ended up discarding. And now we have a new station and turnout gear and, most importantly, our city is now rated as an eight on the fire protection scale. We have been given the go-ahead to get a new fire engine.

Everyone was clapping for we all knew how far we had come, and then Greg started talking about dedication and hard work. He said my name and dubbed me as rookie of the year for nineteen ninety-seven, and it was great. Rusty got fireman of the year. And it was a good night for everyone.

Growing up in Columbus, I have always wanted to be a fireman. I had people that I called heroes like pete Rose and Johnny Bench, just to name a few, but when I met my new dad and uncles, that all changed. I saw the way they would light up the room when they entered, the laughter and the jokes. It was something that, as a kid, I always wanted to be around and a part of. And now I am, and it is great.

We lost my uncle John Henry to cancer in two thousand one. I went to see him with Mom and Dad a week before he died, and the man I had remembered was not the man I saw that day. He weighed ninety pounds, and he was sitting in a chair. I went to him, hugged his neck, and told him that I loved him and would never forget him. He said he loved me too. I could not get over what had happened to him, and I saw my dad cry that day for the first time.

My dad had to drop out of school in the ninth grade to work in the cotton mill after Granddaddy went off to fight in the war. So dad had to make sure they went to school and graduated. I think he felt like a father losing a son. I know that is why I feel very lucky to have had parents like Mom and Dad. They let us be ourselves and enjoy a lot of great things. We were poor and didn't have a lot of things that other kids had, but you would have never known that by the way we lived.

I don't remember a lot about my first few years of life except that my grandmother helped raise my two brothers and me. My mother was always at work in order to provide for the five of us, but I do remember when my mom married my stepdad. And I will never forget the night I got a call from my little brother saying that Daddy was gone.

We always went to see them for their birthdays and anniversary on February 21. Well, this year, that fell on a Wednesday, so we went and ate dinner on the Sunday before instead. I noticed that Dad was not feeling well, but he never lead on that anything was wrong; a head cold was all he told me, nothing to worry about. I told him I loved him and gave him a big hug when I left around five o'clock that afternoon.

They live in Meriwether County, which is about ninety miles from where we live, and it takes about an hour and a half to drive there. I received the phone call around two thirty Monday morning, Lisa and I woke up, and when I hung up, I told her what was going on, and as I walked out the door, she told me to drive carefully.

I looked down at my speed when I was on the interstate, and I was doing one hundred miles an hour. It took me forty-five minutes to get to my parents' house. When I pulled in to the driveway, there was a fire truck already there, and as I walked in the house, the chief of the Meriwether volunteer fire department was there sitting with my mom.

My little brother is a fireman for the volunteer department here in Meriwether County, and as I walked in the bedroom, I saw Daddy on the bed. As I walked over to him, it was quiet.

"It is something we all will have to do some day" is all I could think of because he had told me that when I was young and Granddaddy passed away. Dad had told me that when the time comes, we will know everything or nothing at all, and I can say that my dad knows everything now.

At the funeral I met men that Dad had coached in Little League thirty years before that remembered him telling them to work hard for the things they wanted out of life. And some firemen that knew Daddy, people who had worked with him, and his friends told me he was a very caring man.

I miss my dad every day and wish he was here for when I have questions about how to smoke a Boston butt, or how to tell my kids that Papa is gone to heaven, or just about life in general. He was a big part of my foundation and what I will pass on to my kids. It took me nineteen years before I ever told my dad that I loved him because I thought he knew. But I tell my kids I love them every day just to be sure.

He was sixty-three when he passed, and ten years later, I can still hear him when I think I can't do something, want to quit, or feel alone and scared.

He will say, "pick it up. let's go, son, you can do it." I will just laugh, press on, and say "OK, Dad."

THE REASON

Ask not what your country can do for you. Ask what you can do for your country.

—John Fitzgerald Kennedy

I KNOW EVERYONE in America knows where they were and what they were doing on that September day in two thousand one at eight forty-six in the morning. I was working at the paper mill, and I went in the office to talk to Dwight, and our secretary Mary was watching the small TV that we had in the office. She said, "Come look at this. The twin towers in New York City just got hit by an airplane." I walked in the office and was looking at the TV when the second plane slammed into the south tower at nine-o-three, and I was stunned just watching all the horror and tragedy that was happening. I saw those brave firemen on the way to save and help protect the citizens of New York City. I felt proud to be in the same class as those guys because I know they would do whatever it takes to save and protect anybody that needed help. What we do as firemen is to help the people that need it and risk our lives for our fellow human beings.

As we continued to watch all the confusion and pandamonia going on in the city, it was clear that someone had done this on purpose. We continued to watch, and then it happened. I felt my heart sink as I knew that New York's finest were doing their job when the towers came down on them. I had to walk away because it was like a member of my family had just passed away.

I watched in disbelief that night on the news with my family as they were talking about everything that had happened today. They showed the

NYFD heading into the city and then the twin towers coming down, and they still did not know how many were dead, hurt, or missing.

We heard a few days later when they showed all the numbers of dead and unaccounted for, of my brother firemen and emergency workers. There were four hundred and eleven all total that paid the ultimate price to save their fellow men. They said in the beginning that the hijacked planes took the towers down, but in the end, it was the fire and heat that made them fall.

The next night, I went into town, and we got together at the station and talked about what happened. Everyone started saying if they had done this or that, they would have been safe. And I said, "They've done what they were trained to do and that is saving lives. And they did that to the end."

I could not get the sights out of my head and would catch myself in tears sometimes thinking about what had happened and wondering who would do something like that to hurt so many good people and their families for the rest of their lives. I then started thinking of how I could help my country heal and do my part as a United States citizen, as president Kennedy once said, "Ask not what your country can do for you. .. [but] what you can do for your country".

Three years later I got a job working overseas on building new US embassies and to protect our people overseas from any danger that might arise anywhere in the world, not just here at home but everywhere. It was very hard for me to leave Lumpkin and my fellow firemen that I had a bond with, but they understood and told me they would do the same if given the chance. It was a hard day when I turned in my turnout gear and SCBA and said good-bye to a dream come true, but it has helped me in the long run as to where I've been.

I have worked in Kuwait and Baghdad as a maintenance electrician during "Enduring Freedom" in two thousand nine, the year before Dustin was to graduate from high school. My job was to keep the military men and women comfortable in their offices while they did their jobs of keeping our country safe.

I recall one time when I was working in Kuwait on SpOD (Strategic port of Departure), and being on the night shift, I have to go out to different bases like Camp Arijan, Camp patriot, and Ali Al Salem in the middle of the night to do maintenance on any building that the military is housed in and keep it safe and in working condition. I would fix light fixtures or change out air-conditioning or anything to keep the building operational and safe so the military could comfortably do their jobs.

Some nights it was so dark and windy that the roads disappear right in front of your eyes, and it was a little scary not knowing where to turn in the middle of the desert with no signs or power pole to show you the way. Dustin was playing baseball in high school at this time, and a couple of his teammates' fathers were in the military and stationed at Fort Benning. They had received orders to go to Afghanistan and Saudi Arabia to help win the war and protect our troops.

Mr. Carbone is a good friend of mine, and he helps keep our boys in shape and ready to take on any baseball team in Columbus. We call it the "lt. Colonel Carbone's workouts" at six thirty in the morning before school, which is a great motivator. Craig is a great guy, and he had become a good friend, and I was home for a rest and relaxation around the time the baseball team was cooking Boston butts to raise money for new uniforms and equipment. I helped do some cooking and Mr. Carbone, Craig, and I hung out, and being in January, it was very cold and wet, but we did our part for the boys. We also talked about the war and when I had to go back over to Kuwait, and I told them, "In about two weeks."

Craig also told me that he had gotten his orders to go to Bagram air force base in Afghanistan for a year. I was lucky for my tour was six months, then I would come home for two weeks. Mr. Carbone was home for good and told me to be safe while I was over there. That bothered me because I had heard a lot of stories about the front line and some of the things going on there, and I was afraid for Craig or any military person that had to come over to Iraq or Afghanistan.

A couple of weeks later I got an e-mail from Craig that he would be arriving at Ali Al Salem around the first of the month, and since I worked on the night shift and it was one of the camps I did maintenance on, I could go see him when he got there.

I got the e-mails, and when I went to work that day, I asked George if we had any maintenance reports to go fix anything in Ali Al Salem, and he said, "Yes, an air-conditioner was acting up in the supply connex."

I got the report, and George and I headed out to make the long drive to the base. It was about an hour and a half drive through the desert to the camp, and at night in the desert, it all looked the same, and it was dark.

We made it to the camp, and it took about fifteen minutes to get through security in to the base, which is a good thing.

I drove through the camp to tent number 12, and I could see why they call it Tent City. George and I got to Craig's tent, and it was small, twelve men in a twenty-by-twenty tent.

Craig came out, and I told him, "let's get a cup of coffee at the Green Bean Coffee shack."

We sat around and talked about baseball, the kids, and just life in general. We had some laughs and talked like we were back home until about ten o'clock when we had to walk over to the big tent in the middle of camp to see if Craig was going to ship out that night or have to wait till tomorrow. I was hoping for neither.

We stood around and waited and listened for the names to leave, and luckily, Craig's was not on the list for that night, and I was relieved. We stayed a little longer and took a few pictures, and I told Craig that we had to get back to work. I shook his hand and told him to stay safe and I'd see him back home.

I left that night, and I asked God to watch over my friend because people like Craig are few and far between, and the world would be less of a place to be in if something happened to him because he is truly a "silent guardian."

I got to meet a lot of men and women I call heroes, the men and women that I had the pleasure to help and make a little more comfortable while they fought for our freedom, and the ones that I worked with in maintenance.

I even got to take care of some young guys that patrolled around the pier and kept me and my friend's safe while I was there. One night while I was out checking some perimeter lights around our base, I ran into a couple of young guys from the Alabama National Guard in a Humvee. John and David were about twenty years old, and they reminded me of Dustin. John and I talked about back home, and I found out he is from Alabama and had played baseball in junior college, and I'm from Georgia and love baseball, so we could talk about a lot of similar things.

I asked John what he missed about back home, and he said he would like to have a grillout with hamburgers and hot dogs. And I told him I would see what I could do and let him know.

I went back to the office and sat down with my night supervisor, George, and the power generator guy, Sasha, and we decided to go to the PX in Camp Arijan and get some stuff to surprise the troops the next time they were on the night shift.

It was about a week later and at one o'clock in the morning on a Saturday that we had a cookout, and it was pretty neat. We had some country music playing on the truck radio and were laughing and eating hamburgers and hot dogs. And the guys were parked around us in their Humvees. For a moment, there was no war, and nobody worried about anything except what to put on their hot dog or hamburger, or what chip tasted better with their food. It was great.

I left Kuwait and Iraq after sixteen months and headed to Africa to help build new US embassies and make them safe for our US citizens and young marines around the world. I have meet so many great people in liberia, Rwanda, Burundi, Mali, and Guinea that I am a better person for their friendship.

I remember one friend in Conakry, Guinea, and his name was John. John was a math teacher that had fled liberia with his wife and two daughters and lost everything they had during the civil war there. He was hired to work for our contractor to take care of us and help us with food and anything to make our stay a little better while we built the US embassy there. I got together with the electricians that worked with me, and we decided to make John's life a little better before we left to go home. We gave John enough money to pay for his kids to go to school till they graduated since they don't believe in a child left behind. We also bought his family a house full of furniture, beds, tables, and a couch.

There was also a young man that worked on the embassy in liberia as a mason's helper. He got attacked by a bunch of men, and they stole his phone and beat him up. I helped him by buying him a phone because that was his only communication with his mom in the United States, and he gave me a picture of himself when he graduated and thanked me every day.

I wish I could have helped others, but you can't help everyone, so you help the ones you can. I am happy with my life so far, and I have met a lot of great men and women around the world. I have come to realize that there are people everywhere that, at a moment's notice, will help save a life or put their life in danger for another human being.

We are the same when it comes down to the basic ways of life. We are just trying to make a living the best way we know how and provide for our families and help one another.

And that is what it takes to be a silent guardian.